# HEALTHY HOMEMADE DOG FOOD RECIPES

ALL IN ONE COOKBOOK: EASY TO PREPARE, BUDGET FRIENDLY MEALS, FOR YOUR HAPPY & HEALTHY DOG

## DAKOTA O'HARE

**Publisher's Cataloging-in-Publication Data**
**Title of Work:** Healthy Homemade Dog Food Recipes: All In One Cookbook
**Date of First Publication**: June 17, 2024
**Nation of 1$^{st}$ Publication:** United States
**Author:** John F. Noone
**Pseudonym:** Dakota O'Hare

Healthy Homemade Dog Food Recipes: All In One Cookbook
ASIN: BOD7BRCBQ3 (Paperback)
ASIN: BOD79N73NZ (ePub e-book)
ASIN: BOD7CC2ZBF (Hardcover)
Copyright Office Registration Number: TX 9-408-397
Effective Date of Registration: June 24, 2024

**Rights and Permissions**
**Name:** John F Noone
**Email:** redt3641@gmail.com

# TABLE OF CONTENTS

Introduction                                                    9

1. NUTRITION FOR ALL LIFE STAGES                               13
   1.1 Tailoring Nutrition for Different Dog Life Stages       14
   1.2 Decoding Nutritional Labels: What Every Dog
   Owner Should Know                                           16
   1.3 The Role of Macronutrients: Proteins, Fats, and
   Carbohydrates                                               18
   1.4 Hydration: Ensuring Your Dog Drinks Enough
   Water                                                       19
   1.5 Vitamins and Minerals Essentials for Your Dog          20
   1.6 Understanding Food Allergies and Intolerances
   in Dogs                                                     22

2. LAYING THE GROUNDWORK                                       25
   2.1 Pre-Transition Checklist: Preparing Your Kitchen       26
   2.2 Creating a 4-Week Transition Plan for Your Dog         27
   2.3: Monitoring Your Dog's Health and Adjusting
   Portions                                                    30
   2.4 Identifying and Managing Detox Symptoms                31
   2.5 When to Consult a Veterinarian During Transition       33

3. SOURCING AND SELECTING SUPERIOR
   INGREDIENTS                                                 37
   3.1: Shopping Guide: Where to Buy Quality
   Ingredients                                                 38
   3.2 Budget-Friendly Tips for Buying in Bulk                39
   3.3: Safe Storage and Handling of Ingredients             41
   3.4 Time-Saving Meal Prepping Strategies                   42
   3.5 Creating a Weekly Meal Prep Routine                    44
   3.6 Innovative Freezing and Thawing Techniques for
   Dog Meals                                                   45

4. THE DAWN OF NOURISHMENT                                     47
   4.1: Simple and Nutritious Breakfast Bowls                 48
   4.2 Protein-Packed Dinners for Optimal Health              49

4.3 Healthy Fats and Oils for Coat Shine and Skin
Health     51

4.4 Carb Choices: Safe Vegetables and Fruits     52

4.5 Special Needs Diets: Low-Calorie Meals for
Weight Management     54

4.6 Hydrating Homemade Broths and Soups     55

Healthy Homemade Chicken Recipes for Dogs     57

Sundance's Chicken and Rice Roundup     58

Charlie's Chicken and Pumpkin Stew     59

Bella's Chicken and Sweet Potato Mash     60

Lucy's Chicken Veggie Mash     61

Max's Chicken and Oats Surprise     62

Rusty's Chicken and Lentils Delight     63

Luna's Chicken Pea Pilaf     64

Blackies Chicken and Barley Soup     65

Augie's Chicken Apple Crunch     66

Sadie's Chicken and Veggie Kibble Mix     67

Healthy Homemade Beef Recipes for Dogs     69

Aldo's Beef and Rice Casserole     69

Niki's Hearty Beef Stew     70

Bud's Beefy Barley Bowl     71

Seamus's Beefy Mash     72

Dakota's Nutritious Beef and Veggie Mix     73

Bailey's Beef, Rice, and Pea Patties     74

Molly's Beef and Zucchini Stir-Fry     76

Daisy's Ground Beef and Potato Gratin     77

Coco's Slow-Cooked Beef and Apple Delight     78

Guinness's Beef and Egg Breakfast Scramble     79

Healthy Protein Options for Dogs     80

Healthy Homemade Fish Recipes for Dogs     81

Duke's Simple Fish and Rice     82

Henry's Fish and Sweet Potato Stew     83

Stella's Salmon and Rice Casserole     84

Ellie's Fish Vegetable Medley     85

Tucker's Fish and Egg Scramble     86

Bear's Sardine and Potato Dinner     87

Nola's Salmon and Pea Puree     88

Cooper's Cod and Barley Soup     89

Major's Haddock and Rice Pilaf     90

Finn's Trout and Vegetable Stir-Fry     91

Here are some types of fish that should be avoided in
dog food:     92
Healthy Fruits for Dogs     93
Healthy Vegetables for Dogs     95
Healthy Homemade Dog Treat Recipes     98
Murphy's Peanut Butter Pumpkin Treats     98
Teddy's Sweet Potato and Oats Biscuits     99
Chloe's Apple Carrot Chews     100
Sophie's Chicken and Rice Balls     101
Jack's Beefy Spinach Squares     102
Summer's Delight - Ice Cream for Dogs     103
Toxic Foods and Household Items for Dogs     106

5. TAILORING DIETS FOR THRIVING CANINES     111
   5.1 Anti-Inflammatory Meals for Joint Health     112
   5.2 Gut-Friendly Foods to Improve Digestion     113
   5.3 Boosting Immunity with Antioxidant-Rich
   Recipes     115
   5.4 Canine Detox: Clean Meals to Reset Your Dog's
   Health     117
   5.5 Low-Allergen Meals for Sensitive Dogs     119
   5.6 Recipes to Support Oral Health and Freshen
   Breath     120

6. NURTURING VITALITY WITH NATURE'S BOUNTY     123
   6.1 Superfoods for Dogs: What They Are and How to
   Use Them     124
   6.2 The Benefits of Fermented Foods in a Dog's Diet     125
   6.3 Integrating Herbal Supplements Safely     127
   6.4 The Role of Probiotics and Prebiotics     128
   6.5 Customizing Diets for Athletic and Working Dogs     130
   6.6 Nutrient-Rich Treats and Snacks     132

7. NURTURING ADAPTABILITY IN CANINE DIETS     135
   7.1 Overcoming Picky Eating: Tips and Tricks     136
   7.2 Adjusting Portions for Weight Gain or Loss     137
   7.3 Recognizing and Responding to Food Allergies     140
   7.4 Dealing with Digestive Upsets: Diarrhea and
   Constipation     142
   7.5 Transitioning Senior Dogs to a Homemade Diet     145
   7.6 Balancing Homemade Meals with Occasional
   Commercial Foods     146

8. BUILDING A CIRCLE OF SUPPORT AND
KNOWLEDGE                                                    149
8.1 Forming a Support Network with Fellow Dog
Owners                                                        150
8.2 Staying Informed: Continued Learning about
Canine Nutrition                                             152
8.3 Engaging with Experts: When to Seek Professional
Advice                                                        155
8.4 Documenting Your Dog's Diet and Health
Progress                                                      156
8.5 Advocating for Whole Foods: Educating Others
on Homemade Dog Food Benefits                                158
8.6 Exploring Advanced Canine Nutrition Courses
and Resources                                                160

Conclusion                                                    165
References                                                    169

*This book is dedicated to all of my family and friends and all the dogs we've ever loved.*

# INTRODUCTION

Growing up I was surrounded by the kind of wholesome life many
people dream of. I spent my summers filled with the sights and

sounds of nature. Helping out at my friend's farm with the joyous company of our dogs, who were as much a part of our family as anyone else. These loyal friends rarely ate dog food bought from the store; instead, they thrived on the same fresh, homemade meals that we enjoyed. This wasn't just a lifestyle choice, it was a testament to our belief in the power of whole, natural foods.

Sundance is at the heart of all these memories, a spirited black and white sheepdog with eyes that sparkled with intelligence and vitality. Sundance was more than a pet; he was my constant companion, a vital part of the farm's summer operations, and a good example of the difference a diet of fresh, whole foods can make. Watching him grow, thrive, and work alongside me, I saw firsthand how significant diet is to my dogs' health, happiness, and well-being.

This book is as much Sundance's legacy as it is my own experiences on a farm that was rich in natural food sources to a passionate advocate for canine nutrition. It's a journey that has taught me the importance of every meal we put in front of our furry family members and has inspired me to share this knowledge with others. My goal is to honor Sundance's memory by helping dog owners like you transform their pets' health through simple, nutritious and homemade meals.

"Healthy Homemade Dog Food Recipes: All In One Cookbook" is designed to demystify canine nutrition, making it accessible, affordable and adaptable for every dog owner. Inside, you'll find detailed nutrient and calorie information, a 4-week transition chart for dogs switching from store-bought to homemade food, and sensible guidelines to ensure your dog receives optimal nutrition. My book is about saving time and money without compromising on the quality of your dog's diet, ensuring they enjoy better oral hygiene, healthier skin, and a shinier coat.

I understand the concerns many dog owners have about the time, cost, and complexity of preparing homemade dog food. That's why this book is crafted with your needs in mind, offering practical advice, emotional support, and science-backed nutritional guidelines. It's not just a collection of recipes but a comprehensive guide to strengthening the bond between you and your dog through the food they eat.

Inspired by Sundance's story, let me help you understand and transform the way you think about your dogs' nutrition. Your furry friend's journey to better health and happiness starts here.

# CHAPTER 1
# NUTRITION FOR ALL LIFE STAGES

I n canine care, the dietary needs of a dog change significantly from the puppy phase through adulthood and into the senior years. This evolution isn't merely about increasing or decreasing food portions but involves a balance of nutrients, each step carefully adjusted to the rhythm of life's stages.

## 1.1 TAILORING NUTRITION FOR DIFFERENT DOG LIFE STAGES

### Different Nutritional Needs

The dietary requirements of dogs vary with age, puppies, with their boundless energy and rapid growth rates, have a dietary need for more calories per pound of body weight compared to adult dogs. Meanwhile, adult dogs require a balanced diet that supports maintenance and daily energy needs without promoting obesity. As dogs enter their senior years, their metabolism slows, necessitating fewer calories but a continued emphasis on high-quality, easily digestible nutrients to support aging bodies.

### Life Stage Transitions

Transitioning a dog's diet between life stages is important; timing and adjusting techniques are critical. For instance, puppies weaned off their mother's milk need a gradual introduction to solid foods, starting with easily digestible options and slowly incorporating more variety and solidity as they grow. Similarly, as dogs age into their senior years, their diet may need adjustment to include foods that are easier on the kidneys, with possible supplements to support joint health. These transitions should be gradual, over the course of several days or weeks, to avoid gastrointestinal upset.

### Special Considerations for Growth

During the puppy stage, the emphasis on protein and calcium is paramount, as these are the building blocks for strong bones and muscles. However, an excess, particularly of calcium, can lead to developmental issues in large-breed puppies, a testament to the adage that more isn't always better. The balance is delicate and requires a nuanced approach to ensure puppies grow at an appropriate rate, laying a strong foundation for a healthy adult life.

**Senior Dog Care**

As dogs enter their golden years, their dietary focus shifts toward maintaining health rather than supporting growth. Reduced calorie intake helps manage weight, as obesity can exacerbate common senior dog issues such as arthritis. However, fiber becomes more critical to aid in digestion, and certain nutrients, like omega-3 fatty acids, can support joint health and cognitive function. This phase of life also often brings about a decrease in taste and smell sensitivity, making the palatability of food an important consideration to ensure senior dogs maintain their appetite and nutritional intake.

In drawing parallels between canine nutrition and human dietary needs across different life stages, the importance of tailored nutrition becomes clear. Just as infants have different dietary requirements than teenagers or elderly individuals, so too do puppies, adult dogs, and senior canines, who need specific nutrients to support their health and well-being at each stage of life. This understanding lays the groundwork for a holistic approach to feeding our canine companions, ensuring they receive not just food, but nourishment that promotes a long, healthy, and vibrant life.

Reflecting on this, it becomes evident that the responsibility of caring for a dog is a dynamic, evolving task that demands our attention, knowledge, and adaptability. The commitment to providing the best possible nutrition at every stage of a dog's life is a powerful testament to the bond between humans and their canine companions—a bond built on love, respect, and the mutual desire for a life well-lived.

## 1.2 DECODING NUTRITIONAL LABELS: WHAT EVERY DOG OWNER SHOULD KNOW

In today's world, prioritizing the health and well-being of our dogs is essential. Learning to interpret the complex nutritional labels on dog food packaging goes beyond a mere skill—it becomes an essential part of responsible dog ownership. Beyond the attractive marketing and eye-catching packaging lies vital information needed to make well-informed choices about our dogs' diets. Despite the complexity of this information, with a bit of patience and effort, we can decode this wide array of ingredients and nutritional facts. This process enables us to understand the true quality of the food we give to our beloved pets.

**Understanding Ingredients**

Understanding the sequence of ingredients on a dog food label is crucial; it's not merely a list but a structured order based on the weight of each ingredient. This arrangement provides valuable insights into the formula's composition, with those ingredients appearing first being present in the highest quantities. Such knowledge is key for dog owners to gauge food quality effectively. When a high-quality protein like chicken or beef tops the list, it signals a nutrient-rich product, contrasting significantly with those where grains or fillers dominate. Recognizing this difference is essential, as it influences the health and well-being of dogs across all life stages.

**Identifying Fillers and Additives**

The discernment between necessary nutrients and unnecessary fillers or harmful additives is a critical aspect of analyzing dog food labels. Fillers, often in the form of corn, wheat, and soy, are used to bulk up the food without providing significant nutritional value. While these may not be inherently harmful, their predominance over more nutritious ingredients can compromise the food's overall nutritional profile. Additionally, certain additives, while enhancing flavor, color, or shelf life, may not align with the optimal dietary needs of a dog. Artificial colors, flavors, and preservatives are among those that caring owners should avoid, opting instead for foods that rely on the natural appeal and preservation properties of high-quality ingredients.

## Nutritional Adequacy Statement

Perhaps one of the most telling aspects of a dog food label is the nutritional adequacy statement. This declaration, often overlooked in the shadow of more prominent features, serves as a testament to the food's ability to meet the nutritional standards established by the Association of American Feed Control Officials (AAFCO). This statement is the culmination of rigorous evaluation, indicating whether the food provides a complete and balanced diet for a specific life stage (puppy, adult, senior) or if it's intended for supplemental feeding only. The presence and specificity of this statement are invaluable for owners aiming to ensure their dogs receive nutrition that supports their health and well-being throughout the various phases of life.

## Deciphering Feeding Guidelines

The feeding guidelines, typically found alongside the nutritional adequacy statement, offer a structured approach to determining the appropriate portion sizes for a dog, based on weight and some-times activity level. However, these guidelines are not prescriptive but rather starting points for individual adjustment. Dogs, like people, have unique metabolic rates and nutritional needs influenced by factors such as age, activity level, and health status. The discerning owner can tailor feeding practices to meet their dog's specific requirements, ensuring optimal nutrition and preventing issues related to overfeeding or underfeeding.

Navigating through the maze of ingredients, nutritional adequacy, and feeding guidelines equips owners with the knowledge to make decisions that significantly affect their dogs' well-being. This journey underscores a deep commitment to the health and joy of our canine friends, guaranteeing that the food we offer does more than just satisfy hunger—it supports their overall vitality and contributes to their happiness, sparking the lively spirit that brings so much joy to our lives.

## 1.3 THE ROLE OF MACRONUTRIENTS: PROTEINS, FATS, AND CARBOHYDRATES

In the world of dog nutrition, proteins are fundamental, acting as crucial building blocks for muscle development and repair, and enhancing the immune system to fend off health issues. These essential nutrients, derived from both animal and plant sources, are pivotal for the maintenance and growth of your dog's muscles, ensuring they have the strength and endurance needed for their daily activities. Proteins are particularly vital for dogs in their growth phase or those with high physical demands, supporting their energy needs and overall health.

Fats, on the other hand, play a significant role in your dog's diet by providing a rich source of energy and aiding in the absorption of vital fat-soluble vitamins such as A, D, E, and K. These nutrients are essential for healthy cells, nerves, and muscles. Omega-3 and omega-6 fatty acids, commonly found in fish oils, are key to minimizing inflammation, which benefits the skin and coat health of your dog. The right balance of fats not only supports their energetic needs but also contributes to their internal and external health.

Carbohydrates, despite some skepticism, are an important part of a dog's diet, offering fiber and energy. Found in vegetables, fruits, and grains, carbohydrates aid in digestive health by supporting regular bowel movements and providing a vital source of glucose for brain function and energy. They play a role in maintaining your dog's energy and cognitive functions, especially during times of lower food intake. Additionally, carbohydrates help nurture a healthy gut microbiota, which is crucial for optimal nutrient absorption and a strong immune system.

Understanding the balance of these macronutrients is key to providing a nutritious diet tailored to your dog's specific needs, which may vary based on age, breed, activity level, and health conditions. For example, an active working dog might need a diet higher in proteins and fats to support their energy and muscle repair needs, while a more sedentary, older dog might benefit from a calorie-controlled diet rich in nutrients to support joint health and weight management. This balance should be flexible, adapting to the changing nutritional needs of your dog throughout their life stages. Creating a well-balanced diet for your dog is an act of love and care, reflecting our commitment to their health and happiness.

By focusing on a diet rich in essential macronutrients, we can support their well-being and vitality for the long term. This approach to nutrition underscores the deep bond we share with our dogs, rooted in mutual respect and the joy of a shared life, highlighting that macronutrients are more than just dietary components; they represent our dedication to nourishing our canine companions in every sense.

## 1.4 HYDRATION: ENSURING YOUR DOG DRINKS ENOUGH WATER

Hydration is a crucial yet often overlooked aspect of dog health. Water is essential for all life forms, including dogs, as it supports vital biological functions and helps maintain optimal organ performance and body temperature regulation. The importance of hydration goes beyond just satisfying thirst; it's a foundational element of overall health. Dog owners should be vigilant for signs of dehydration, which can include decreased playfulness, dull eyes, dry gums, reduced skin elasticity, and lethargy. Recognizing these early signs is key to preventing more serious health issues. Encouraging dogs to drink enough can be challenging, particularly for those who seem indifferent to their water bowls.

However, ensuring the freshness and cleanliness of their water can significantly influence their drinking habits. Regularly changing the water and cleaning the bowl can encourage even the most hesitant dogs to drink. Having multiple water stations in the home and yard, as well as carrying a portable water dish on walks and trips, can also help keep them hydrated.

Incorporating homemade meals into your dog's diet is another effective way to increase their water intake. Using ingredients with high moisture content, such as watermelon, cucumbers, and zucchini, can subtly boost the hydration levels in their food. Additionally, offering broths and soups as treats or mixing them with dry food can be an appealing way for dogs to consume more liquids. The responsibility of monitoring and promoting adequate hydration is ongoing for dog caregivers.

Understanding that water is not just an addition to their diet but a critical component of their health will influence how we care for them. Providing water, therefore, becomes more than a daily task—it's an expression of the deep bond between humans and their canine companions, rooted in a commitment to their well-being and nurtured by the shared life-giving essence of water.

## 1.5 VITAMINS AND MINERALS ESSENTIALS FOR YOUR DOG

In the realm of canine nutrition, the significance of vitamins and minerals cannot be overstated, despite their requirement in only small quantities. These nutrients are fundamental to a host of bodily functions, including but not limited to, fortifying bones and safeguarding cellular integrity. Vitamins such as A, B, C, D, E, and K, alongside minerals like calcium, phosphorus, and magnesium, are indispensable for the vitality, health, and longevity of our dogs.

Vitamin A plays a crucial role in vision and growth, besides being vital for skin health and immune function. It is readily available in liver, fish oils, and eggs. The B vitamins are pivotal for metabolism and energy production, found in meats, whole grains, and beans, with each type from thiamine (B1) to cobalamin (B12) playing a unique part in supporting the body's energetic demands.

Although dogs can synthesize Vitamin C, its supplementation through fruits and vegetables aids tissue repair and oxidative stress mitigation. Vitamin D is essential for mineral balance, promoting bone and dental health, sourced naturally from sunlight, fish, and fortified foods. Vitamin E, found in vegetable oils, nuts, and greens, acts as an antioxidant, protecting cellular fats and supporting muscle and nerve function. Vitamin K, critical for blood clotting, can be found in leafy greens, kelp, and fish meal, ensuring rapid healing of wounds.

Minerals like calcium, and phosphorus are crucial for building and maintaining a robust skeletal structure, with dairy products, bones, and fish providing a balanced supply. Magnesium, essential for heart and muscle function, is derived from nuts, whole grains, and greens, supporting vital bodily movements. The efficacy of vitamins and minerals greatly depends on their sources, with natural foods offering a bioavailable matrix that enhances nutrient absorption. Liver and eggs are prime examples, rich in essential vitamins while being highly palatable to dogs. However, not all dogs' dietary needs can be met through food alone, necessitating supplements to address any deficiencies without risking excess.

Water-soluble vitamins are generally safer in higher doses due to renal excretion, while fat-soluble vitamins demand caution to avoid toxicity. Supplementation should be considered carefully, possibly under veterinary advice, especially for dogs with specific health issues, dietary restrictions, or those of advanced age. A diet rich in variety may suffice for many, but for others, supplements may be necessary to achieve nutritional balance.

Ultimately, the aim is to support and enhance our dogs' health through careful dietary choices, monitoring, and, when needed, supplementation. By doing so, we honor the commitment to our canine companions' well-being, providing not just nourishment but a foundation for a life filled with energy, happiness, and the special moments that enrich our shared existence.

## 1.6 UNDERSTANDING FOOD ALLERGIES AND INTOLERANCES IN DOGS

Navigating the world of canine nutrition requires careful attention to food allergies and intolerances, which can significantly impact our dogs' health and comfort. These reactions, though different in their underlying causes, present a range of symptoms that can disrupt a dog's well-being. Allergies result from the immune system's response to a perceived threat from certain proteins, while intolerances involve digestive issues without an immune reaction. Recognizing and addressing these issues is crucial for maintaining the health of our furry friends.

Common allergens in dogs include beef, dairy, wheat, chicken, eggs, and soy—ingredients frequently found in commercial dog foods. These can unwittingly become sources of discomfort for our pets, making it our responsibility to identify and avoid these triggers. The symptoms of food allergies and intolerances can vary but often manifest as itchy skin, ear infections, vomiting, diarrhea, and lethargy. Persistent symptoms, especially when linked to a consistent diet, may indicate a food-related issue. Itchy skin, digestive problems, and a general state of discomfort often prompt further investigation into a dog's diet.

An elimination diet is a reliable method to identify food sensitivities. This diet involves feeding the dog a simplified diet of novel proteins and carbohydrates it hasn't encountered before. Over time, this helps reset the dog's system, allowing symptoms to diminish. Following this period, individual ingredients are slowly reintroduced to determine which ones may be causing reactions. This careful, step-by-step process helps to pinpoint specific dietary triggers and develop a meal plan that avoids them. Long-term management of food allergies and intolerances involves vigilance and adaptability. Insights from the elimination diet guide future food choices, whether that means selecting specialized commercial diets or preparing homemade meals that avoid known allergens.

Supplements may also be necessary to ensure nutritional needs are met despite dietary restrictions. However, managing a dog's diet extends beyond their meals. Treats, medications, and even incidental contact with allergenic foods can pose risks. Owners must be vigilant about all aspects of their dog's environment to prevent accidental exposure to allergens. Effective management of food allergies and intolerances also relies on communication with veterinarians, nutritionists, and other dog owners facing similar challenges. Sharing experiences and solutions can offer support and lead to innovative approaches to managing these conditions. Addressing food allergies and intolerances in dogs is a journey from uncertainty to understanding. It's a commitment to our dogs' health and happiness, ensuring they lead comfortable and joyful lives.

# CHAPTER 2
# LAYING THE GROUNDWORK

A s the day begins to break, there's a special kind of preparation taking place in the kitchens of dog owners who choose the path of making homemade dog food. This task, simple at first glance, holds the power to revolutionize your dog's health and happiness. The key to this transformation is not found in elaborate actions but in careful attention to detail and a deep understanding of what you're undertaking. It's similar to how a gardener prepares the soil before planting seeds, making sure everything is perfectly set for growth and prosperity. In this light, the kitchen transforms from a mere space for cooking into a haven of health, where every tool and technique is thoughtfully chosen to enrich the life of your treasured dog.

## 2.1 PRE-TRANSITION CHECKLIST: PREPARING YOUR KITCHEN

### Essential Kitchen Tools

Embarking on this admirable journey starts with a careful selection of kitchen tools and equipment, each chosen for its role in making meal prep both efficient and nutritious. A top-notch food processor or blender is crucial for pureeing vegetables, grinding meats, and mixing ingredients into a smooth, dog-friendly concoction. Likewise, sturdy cutting boards and sharp knives are necessary for finely chopping ingredients to the right size and consistency. Accurate measuring cups and spoons, along with mixing bowls, are invaluable for maintaining the right proportions and balance, aiding in the creation of wholesome meals.

### Organizing Your Space

Once the kitchen tools are ready, the next step is to efficiently organize your kitchen space. Think of your kitchen as a well-organized library where every item has its place and is easily accessible when needed. Store ingredients by their type and how often you use them, ensuring they're clearly labeled to prevent any mix-ups. Keep your countertops clean and clear. This orderly environment fosters creativity, transforming meal preparation from a mundane task into a loving gesture for your pet.

**Safety First**

Dedication to safety kicks off with mastering food handling practices: ensuring hands and surfaces are washed thoroughly

This will ensure they are fresh and of high quality, steering clear of anything that appears spoiled or contaminated.

**Creating a Meal Prep Schedule**

Creating a meal prep schedule is crucial to streamlining your kitchen for homemade dog food preparation, highlighting the importance of managing time effectively. By establishing a routine that aligns with your daily life, you can set aside specific times for preparing and storing your dog's meals, preventing the process from becoming a daunting task. Such integration ensures that feeding your dog homemade meals becomes a seamless and enjoyable part of your routine, reflecting your deep care and affection. This journey begins in the quiet, purposeful moments spent in the kitchen, where the commitment to your dog's health and happiness takes root.

## 2.2 CREATING A 4-WEEK TRANSITION PLAN FOR YOUR DOG

Switching your dog to a homemade diet is a major shift in their nutritional care, demanding a deliberate and step-by-step method to nurture a smooth transition. This four-week plan is designed to guide you and your dog through this important change. The strategy for this transition is based on a solid understanding of how dogs' bodies work and the importance of slowly introducing new types of food.

## Week-by-Week Guidelines

The first week serves as a gentle introduction, where the home-made diet constitutes a mere 25% of your dog's total food intake, effortlessly mingling with the 75% portion of their customary, store-bought food. This cautious start is designed to gently acclimate your dog's digestive system to new food varieties, thereby miti-gating any potential discomfort while simultaneously ensuring a well-rounded diet.

In the second week, the homemade diet will increase to 50% of your dog's total food intake, combining it with the 50% portion of their customary, store-bought food.

Then, in the third week, the homemade diet will account for 75% of your dog's total food intake and 25% of their customary, store-bought food.

And finally, in the fourth week, the homemade diet will increase to 100% of your dog's total food intake.

This phased increment not only eases your dog's digestive adapta-tion but also provides you an opportunity to observe and assess their response to the dietary transformation.

## Monitoring Reactions

Observing your dog's behavior, appetite, energy levels, and stool quality offers valuable insights into how well they are adjusting to the new diet. Any signs of digestive discomfort, such as increased flatulence, diarrhea, or constipation, warrant attention and may indicate the need for a slower transition. Equally, a keen eye should be kept on your dog's enthusiasm for the new meals, as this can serve as an indicator of palatability and acceptance. Keeping a detailed journal during this period, noting both the positive and negative responses, becomes an invaluable tool, allowing for an objective assessment of the transition's progress.

## Adjusting the Plan as Needed

The notion that one size fits all is absent in this approach, giving way to a plan that adapts to the feedback you observed. Should signs of digestive discomfort arise, it may become necessary to extend the duration of the transition, perhaps adding an additional week or two to allow your dog's system to adjust more comfortably. Similarly, if certain ingredients appear to be poorly tolerated, they can be substituted for alternatives that may be more agreeable to your dog's digestive system. This flexibility ensures that the transition is not only successful but also meets the unique needs of your dog, prioritizing their comfort and health above all else.

## Consulting with a Vet

Throughout this transition, the guidance of a veterinarian remains an indispensable resource. Before beginning the switch, a consultation can provide a health check to ensure your dog is in a suitable condition for the dietary change. This professional oversight continues to be crucial throughout the transition, offering a medical perspective on any reactions observed and advising on adjustments to the plan as necessary. The veterinarian's expertise, when combined with your observations and care, creates a complete support system for your dog, ensuring the transition is not only smooth but also agreeable to their long-term health and well-being.

While introducing a homemade diet to your dog, each phase, marked by careful observation and adjustment, recognizes the individuality of each dog and the importance of their comfort and health. This steady transition, supported by professional guidance, ensures that the switch to homemade food is not just a change in diet but a step towards a healthier, happier life for your canine companion.

## 2.3: MONITORING YOUR DOG'S HEALTH AND ADJUSTING PORTIONS

Monitoring your dog's health goes beyond simple observation; it's about developing a deep connection with your pet. Paying close attention to subtle changes in your dog's coat, energy levels, and stool quality can reveal a lot about their well-being and dietary needs. These silent signals guide us in fine-tuning our furry friends' meals to meet their changing nutritional requirements.

The sheen of a dog's coat serves as a mirror for the adequacy of their diet. A shiny, robust fur not only enchants the eye but also signals a body well-fed with essential fatty acids, proteins, and vitamins, each contributing to the vitality displayed. While a dull coat suggests nutritional gaps, urging a reassessment of the diet to incorporate more nutrient-dense foods.

Energy levels fluctuate with the ebb and flow of daily life, yet sustained changes signal shifts in dietary needs. A boundless vigor, the hallmark of a well-nourished dog, celebrates the harmony of a balanced diet, while lethargy, subtle in its onset, suggests misalignment. This decrease in vitality, especially notable in dogs once brimming with energy, necessitates a review of calorie intake and nutritional composition. Perhaps the introduction of more complex carbohydrates for sustained energy release or an increase in protein for muscle support. Each adjustment, fine-tuned to the dog's response, seeks to spark a spark of vitality dimmed by dietary inadequacies.

Stool quality offers insights profound in their implications. The consistency, frequency, and appearance of a dog's excrement serve as a direct reflection of their digestive health and the appropriateness of their diet. Firm, well-formed stools indicate a diet well assimilated, while deviations such as looseness or an increased frequency point to potential intolerances or imbalances. This unspoken language of the body calls for dietary analysis, perhaps a reduction of certain ingredients or the introduction of probiotics to support gut health. The caregiver, therefore, fine-tunes their dog's diet with careful consideration, striving for a balance that promotes seamless digestion.

The interplay between health signals and nutritional adjustments is crucial, with regular weight checks playing an indispensable role. These checks are simple yet essential, grounding the dietary management process by offering a clear picture of the dog's physical well-being. The impartial readings from the scale expose the effects of dietary choices, highlighting when it's necessary to modify meal portions based on the dog's activity level, age, and general health. A gain in weight might necessitate smaller portions or a switch to leaner protein sources, whereas weight loss could indicate the need for more calorie-rich meals. This continuous evaluation ensures a balanced diet, maintaining the dog's health at an optimal level.

In this process of observation and adjustment, each action is guided by a keen awareness of canine health, fostering a deeper connection between dog and caregiver. Feeding transforms into an act of love, reflecting the strong bond they share.

## 2.4 IDENTIFYING AND MANAGING DETOX SYMPTOMS

Switching your dog's diet to include homemade meals initiates a natural adjustment process in their body, often described as detoxification. This process, which signals the shift to cleaner, more nutritious food, can lead to various physical symptoms as the body begins to expel built-up toxins. Recognizing and managing these symptoms is essential to supporting your dog comfortably through this period of dietary change.

Detox symptoms can manifest in various ways, commonly appearing as changes in skin and coat, such as more frequent shedding or the development of temporary rashes, as the body begins to eliminate toxins through its largest organ. You might also notice gastrointestinal changes, with slight variations in stool consistency or frequency, which reflect the digestive system's adjustment to the new diet's composition and nutrient levels. Occasionally, dogs may experience a brief dip in energy or minor behavioral shifts, indicative of the body's natural rebalancing and rejuvenation efforts. While these symptoms may initially cause concern, they actually demonstrate the body's inherent healing processes activating in response to a cleaner, more natural diet.

Addressing detox symptoms effectively requires a balanced approach, combining careful at-home care with alert monitoring to determine if a visit to the vet is called for. To soothe mild skin issues, engage in regular grooming and use mild, natural shampoos for baths to lessen discomfort and help remove loose fur, thus promoting skin health. Adding foods high in digestible fiber to your dog's diet can help stabilize digestive functions, gently aiding the system's adjustment. It's also crucial to ensure your dog stays well-hydrated during this time, as a good fluid intake helps in detoxifying the body, benefiting kidney function and overall health.

The severity and duration of detox symptoms can differ greatly from one dog to another, influenced by various factors including age, overall health, and diet before making the switch. Generally, these symptoms are temporary, often appearing subtly within the first few weeks after transitioning to homemade meals and gradually subsiding as the dog's body adapts to the healthier food options. In most cases, these mild symptoms resolve on their own as the detox process naturally concludes. However, if these symptoms worsen or continue longer than expected, it's crucial to consult with a veterinarian. A professional evaluation can help differentiate between typical detox reactions and more serious health concerns that may need medical attention.

During this adjustment phase, the importance of patience cannot be overstated. It serves as a gentle reminder of the time and dedication required for genuine healing and adaptation. Watching your dog closely, with understanding and empathy, and acknowledging the significant changes their body is going through to achieve a healthier state is crucial.

Navigating the subtleties of detox symptoms requires a blend of knowledge, attentiveness, and thoughtful care. By identifying the signs, understanding their causes, and implementing suitable care strategies, you ensure this adjustment period positively impacts your dog's health. Adopting an approach that combines home remedies with professional advice when needed highlights your dedication to the health and happiness for your dog as they shift to a homemade diet. This approach not only supports your dog through the transition but also strengthens your bond, affirming a mutual commitment to a healthier, more vibrant life together.

## 2.5 WHEN TO CONSULT A VETERINARIAN DURING TRANSITION

Transitioning your dog to a homemade diet is a complex process, where the expertise of a veterinarian becomes invaluable, offering guidance and confidence. This collaboration, rooted in a mutual commitment to your dog's health, is especially critical during dietary changes.

**Red Flags: Identifying Situations and Symptoms That Warrant Immediate Veterinary Consultation**

Being attentive to any shifts in your dog's health and behavior, even the minor ones, is essential in protecting their welfare during the dietary transition. Watch for clear indicators such as increased tiredness, sudden changes in eating habits, ongoing digestive issues, or new allergic symptoms. These signs could signal that your dog is not adapting well to the dietary changes or may have other health problems that are just beginning to surface. Acting quickly on these observations is a testament to your dedication to your dog's health, making sure you adjust their diet or address any rising health issues without delay.

### Regular Check-ups: The Importance of Regular Veterinary Check-ups During and After the Dietary Transition

Regular veterinary check-ups are a cornerstone of a smooth dietary transition, serving not just as a health assessment but as a source of reassurance. These consultations are vital for confirming that your dog's health remains uncompromised. During these visits, your vet will check your dog's weight, assess their overall condition, and conduct blood tests to ensure the diet maintains nutritional balance, making adjustments to the meal plan where necessary. These appointments act as significant milestones and provide peace of mind, affirming your dog's health and well-being through professional oversight.

### Seeking Nutritional Advice: Utilizing Veterinary Expertise to Ensure Your Homemade Diet Meets All of Your Dog's Nutritional Needs

The foundation of this joint effort is rooted in tapping into the veterinarian's knowledge to ensure your homemade dog food is nutritionally complete. Their expertise is key in making sure the diet you craft perfectly balances the necessary vitamins, minerals, and macronutrients your dog needs. This collaborative exchange may lead to your vet recommending dietary tweaks, advising on supplements to fill any nutritional voids, or even offering recipes tailored to your dog's specific health requirements. Through this ongoing conversation, what starts as a simple homemade diet evolves into a scientifically backed nutrition plan, meticulously crafted to bolster your dog's health and energy.

As this chapter on navigating your dog's dietary transition concludes, collaboration with veterinary experts, and a dedication to fulfilling our dogs' dietary requirements is essential. Despite the obstacles, our motivation is fueled by our profound affection for our pets and a desire for their enduring health and joy. With a strong foundation set and guided by expert advice, we are ready to explore the vast array of homemade dog food recipes awaiting us, strengthened by the insights and collaborations we've nurtured.

# CHAPTER 3
# SOURCING AND SELECTING SUPERIOR INGREDIENTS

I n a world overflowing with choices, the importance of choosing the right ingredients for your dog's homemade food can't be overstated. It resembles the process of picking the perfect peach from a pile, where you assess its weight, examine its color, and smell its scent to ensure it delivers the delicious taste you expect. This chapter explores the key methods for finding and selecting the freshest and most nutritious components essential to your dog's diet.

## 3.1: SHOPPING GUIDE: WHERE TO BUY QUALITY INGREDIENTS

Choosing the right ingredients is crucial—they don't just improve a meal; they completely transform it. Start by identifying what makes ingredients high-quality and suitable for your dog's diet. Freshness is key: vegetables should be brightly colored and crisp, meats must smell fresh and have a natural color, and grains need to be dry and free of mold. Meeting these standards ensures the food maintains its nutritional value, providing your dog with a wide range of vitamins, minerals, and essential nutrients.

**Local Sourcing Options**

Exploring local sources reveals a wealth of ingredient choices, each benefiting from minimal transportation and maximum freshness. Farmers' markets and cooperative stores emerge as culinary havens. These venues offer seasonal fruits, vegetables, and meats sourced from nearby farms, not only bolstering local agriculture but also ensuring that the ingredients retain their nutritional value thanks to shorter travel times. Conversations with local producers provide insights into their agricultural practices, allowing you to select ingredients that align with your criteria for organic and ethically produced food.

**Online Resources**

For those unique or hard-to-find ingredients not available locally, turning to reputable online vendors can be a game-changer. These online marketplaces, known for their vast selection of bulk, organic, or specialty items, do not sacrifice quality. They connect you with products geared towards sustainable farming and direct-from-producer offerings, such as grass-fed meats, organic grains, and non-GMO vegetables—key elements for a nutritious homemade dog diet. It's important to select sources that are honest about their sourcing practices and have a track record of positive feedback from customers, ensuring the high quality of their offerings.

**Seasonal Shopping Tips**

Selecting ingredients in tune with the seasons not only guarantees their utmost freshness but also enhances affordability. The abundance of seasonal produce, at its nutritional peak, typically results in lower prices due to its plentiful supply. By incorporating these seasonal treasures into your dog's diet, you create a menu that is both diverse and nutrient-dense. This method promotes a seamless connection with nature, enriching your dog's meals with a variety of foods that bolster their health and vitality.

## 3.2 BUDGET-FRIENDLY TIPS FOR BUYING IN BULK

Buying ingredients in bulk for your dog's homemade meals is a smart and forward-thinking strategy. It's not just about saving money; it's about planning ahead for your dog's nutritional needs in a way that's both economical and environmentally friendly. By choosing to buy in larger quantities, you're not only catering to your pet's immediate dietary needs but also ensuring their continued health and happiness. This approach goes beyond simple cost-cutting, embracing a more efficient and sustainable way of meal preparation that benefits both you and your dog.

**Storage Solutions**

The success of storing bulk-purchased ingredients depends on choosing the right storage solutions to maintain their freshness and nutritional integrity. Different ingredients require different storage methods. For example, airtight containers are perfect for keeping grains and dried goods safe from moisture and pests. For meats and other perishables, vacuum-sealed bags can significantly extend their life in the freezer. Meanwhile, herbs and supplements are best stored in hermetic glass jars, which not only help in preserving their freshness but also facilitate clear labeling and easy access. Such thoughtful storage strategies ensure that the bulk ingredients you buy serve as a continuous source of nourishment rather than ending up as waste, demonstrating the importance of organization and planning in maximizing the benefits of bulk buying.

**Avoiding Waste**

The concern over waste is significant when purchasing in bulk, urging pet owners to use their resources wisely and deliberately. To counteract this, adopting strategies like creative meal planning and efficient ingredient usage can turn potential waste into a valuable resource. By setting up a rotation for ingredients based on their expiration dates, perishable items are used promptly in a variety of healthy meals, ensuring nothing goes to waste before losing its nutritional value.

Additionally, batch cooking allows for the conversion of bulk purchases into meals ready to be frozen and served later, optimizing resource use and offering our dogs a diverse menu of nutritious options. This proactive and considerate method guarantees that the benefits of bulk buying are fully leveraged, with every ingredient playing a role in supporting the health and well-being of our canine companions.

## 3.3: SAFE STORAGE AND HANDLING OF INGREDIENTS

Diligence ensures the vitality and safety of the meals you lovingly craft, serving as a bulwark against the invisible threats that can compromise the quality of your dog's diet and, by extension, their health.

### Proper Refrigeration

Your refrigerator and freezer are key to keeping both raw ingredients and prepared meals fresh and nutritious for your dog. Understanding your fridge's different temperature zones can help ensure that fruits, vegetables, and dairy products stay fresh longer. Meats should be stored separately on the bottom shelf to maintain cooler temperatures and reduce the risk of bacterial growth. By freezing meals in individual portions, you not only extend their shelf life, but also make thawing more convenient, preserving the nutritional value of each meal. The freezer, therefore, is not just a tool for convenience but also a protector of your homemade dog food's quality, ensuring the efforts you put into your dog's meals are well preserved.

### Preventing Cross-Contamination

In your kitchen, it's crucial to keep cross-contamination at bay. This hidden risk can affect the safety of your homemade dog food, but you can avoid it by following both traditional and scientific methods. Use separate cutting boards for meats and vegetables to prevent raw and cooked foods from coming into contact. This ensures their paths remain separate, preserving both safety and harmony in your food preparation. Utensils should be thoroughly cleaned with hot, soapy water after each use to remove any residue from raw ingredients. This practice, maintained with every meal preparation, builds a shield of safety against potential hazards, protecting the health of your beloved pet.

**Handling Tips**

The transformation of raw ingredients into meals that nourish and delight your canine companion demands a touch that is both gentle and guided by knowledge. Raw meats, the cornerstone of many nutritious meals, must be handled in a way that respects their potential, both for survival and for harm. Thawing, a process best undertaken in the refrigerator's cold confines, ensures a gradual return to pliability, minimizing the risk of bacterial growth that warmth encourages. This slow process, while testing patience, speaks to a commitment to safety; each hour in the cold is a step towards a meal both delicious and devoid of danger. Once thawed, these ingredients, now ready to fulfill their nutritional destiny, are transformed under the heat of your stove or oven, the raw becoming cooked, and the potential becoming actual in the form of meals that sustain and protect your beloved pet.

## 3.4 TIME-SAVING MEAL PREPPING STRATEGIES

In our busy lives, making homemade dog food requires a thoughtful pause and a rethinking of our daily routines to introduce efficiency to this important task. This shift from simple routine adjustment to a meaningful ritual incorporates time-saving techniques into the meal prep process, making every minute in the kitchen count for your dog's benefit.

**Batch Cooking**

Batch cooking stands as a pivotal element of efficient meal preparation, where you cook meals in bulk to save for later. Imagine setting aside a few hours to whip up a range of dishes, all customized to meet your dog's dietary needs and tastes. Suddenly, your freezer becomes a rich reserve of ready-to-use meals. This approach not only simplifies the feeding routine but also enriches your dog's diet with variety, making sure every meal is as enjoyable as it is healthy.

## Prep Day Planning

Designating a specific day for meal prep transforms your kitchen into a dedicated space for making your dog's meals. This day allows for a concentrated effort on meal preparation, turning what could be seen as a task into an enjoyable activity. Ingredients, thoughtfully selected beforehand, are used to their full potential in recipes that are both nutritious and filled with love. The careful planning of this day goes beyond just deciding what to make; it involves organizing your workspace, ingredients, and cooking utensils for maximum efficiency and flow. This preparation ensures that the process of making your dog's meals is smooth and enjoyable, emphasizing the care and thought put into each dish.

## Efficient Cooking Techniques

Some methods shine for their dual benefits of enhancing flavor while cutting down on time spent in the kitchen. The pressure cooking technique emerges as a key player, swiftly softening even the hardest cuts of meat, a task that would take hours by conventional means. Conversely, slow cooking offers a hands-off approach, slowly melding flavors and textures into rich, satisfying dishes with barely any effort from your side. These methods, distinct in their approach yet unified in their outcomes, pave the way to crafting meals that are both delicious and time-efficient, honoring your schedule as well as your dog's dietary enjoyment.

## Pre-prepared Ingredient Kits

The strategy of assembling pre-prepared ingredient kits elevates meal prep to a new level of convenience and readiness. Imagine neatly arranged containers or bags, each filled with the exact amounts of prepped ingredients required for your recipes. This method significantly streamlines the cooking process. It eliminates the repetitive tasks of measuring, chopping, and organizing ingredients for each meal. By preparing these ingredient kits during quieter times, you infuse your meal prep routine with efficiency and fluidity, allowing for quick and seamless dish assembly. This not only enhances your kitchen productivity but also guarantees that each meal is crafted to meet your dog's dietary requirements.

## 3.5 CREATING A WEEKLY MEAL PREP ROUTINE

Establishing a weekly meal prep routine offers a wealth of benefits, blending practicality with personal care. It creates a dedicated slot in your weekly schedule for your pet's health and well-being. Committing this time turns meal prep into a habit, steering you away from the less healthy, convenient options. It also adds a layer of excitement and ritual to feeding times, transforming it from a simple daily task into a meaningful moment of connection. For your dog, the consistency of their meals fosters a sense of stability and deepens their trust in you, thanks to the dependable provision of thoughtfully prepared food.

Incorporating a variety of meals into your weekly meal prep routine is essential for preventing dietary boredom and keeping your dog eager about mealtime. This can be easily achieved by rotating protein sources, introducing a range of vegetables, and experimenting with different grains or legumes. Each meal then becomes more than just nourishment; it turns into an exploration of tastes and textures for your dog. By selecting recipes that utilize seasonal ingredients, you not only diversify your dog's diet but also enhance its nutritional value. Every ingredient, at its seasonal peak, contributes a unique set of vitamins, minerals, and flavors, enriching your dog's meals. This strategy ensures your dog's diet remains interesting and nutritionally balanced, reflecting a holistic approach to their health and wellbeing.

The invitation extended to family members to participate in the meal preparation process transforms this routine into a shared endeavor, making the kitchen a space of collective action. Assigning tasks, from chopping vegetables to portioning out meals, not only distributes the workload but also fosters a sense of shared responsibility and care for the family pet. For children, this involvement serves as an invaluable lesson in the importance of nutrition and the responsibilities of pet ownership; their contributions are acknowledged as vital to the well-being of their furry sibling. This collaborative approach strengthens family's fabric, with each member's efforts woven together in the shared goal of nurturing their beloved pet. The meals, thus prepared, carry within them the warmth of communal effort, each bite is a reminder of the love and care that sustains their household.

## 3.6 INNOVATIVE FREEZING AND THAWING TECHNIQUES FOR DOG MEALS

Freezing homemade dog meals goes beyond simple storage; it's a deliberate technique that locks in the freshness, taste, and nutritional value, turning your freezer into a treasure chest of healthy meals. When done correctly, this method makes every bit of effort you put into preparing your dog's food pay off, enhancing their health and joy. Freezing isn't just about lowering the temperature; it's about understanding how cold can serve as a guardian of your meal's quality, ensuring that your labor of love keeps its value over time.

Incorporating portion control into your freezing routine elevates it from a mere dietary tool to a key part of your meal preservation strategy. This method simplifies mealtime by dividing the food into individual portions that cater to your dog's specific size and nutritional requirements before freezing. It not only makes thawing and serving more convenient but it also reduces the food's exposure to air and temperature changes each time you open the freezer. Opting for portion-sized containers or vacuum-sealed bags can further minimize freezer burn and keep each meal as fresh and nutritious as the day it was made.

Thawing your dog's carefully frozen meals requires the same level of attention and care as during preparation and freezing. Adhering to proper thawing protocols is critical to keeping each meal safe and nutritionally sound. The best practice is to move the meal from the freezer to the fridge, letting it thaw slowly over a few hours or throughout the night. This gradual thaw ensures the meal retains its original texture and flavor while significantly reducing the risk of harmful bacteria growth that could occur with sudden temperature shifts.

Moving beyond the foundational methods of freezing and thawing, we venture into a creative territory that can elevate both the convenience and attractiveness of homemade dog meals. By employing innovative freezing techniques like utilizing ice cube trays for crafting treats or portioning small meal servings, we introduce a blend of fun and functionality into the meal prep process. These compact, rapidly thawable servings are perfect for offering a cool treat on warm days or for seamlessly integrating a variety of nutrients into your dog's diet without needing to defrost a larger portion. Freezing broth or blended vegetables in these small formats provides a straightforward way to boost your dog's daily hydration and micronutrient levels, while the unique shapes and textures make mealtime more engaging. This inventive freezing strategy not only optimizes your freezer space but also diversifies your dog's meals with little extra effort.

# CHAPTER 4
# THE DAWN OF
# NOURISHMENT

A s dawn breaks and the world awakens, we're presented with
a unique opportunity to influence the day ahead. This tran-

quil time, still untouched by the day's chaos, is perfect for making choices that will define our path forward. When it comes to feeding our beloved dogs, this isn't just about satisfying hunger—it's about seizing the chance to kickstart their day with energy and vitality. The first meal of the day, often rushed or overlooked, is crucial. It's more than a simple routine; it's a critical foundation for our pets' health and well-being that echoes throughout the day.

## 4.1: SIMPLE AND NUTRITIOUS BREAKFAST BOWLS

### Quick and Easy Recipes

In the calm of the early morning, when every minute is valuable, the thought of making a nutritious breakfast for your dog might feel overwhelming. However, simplicity and nutrition can go hand in hand. Imagine a mix of cooked, lean chicken, cubed sweet potatoes, and a sprinkle of blueberries. This trio can be prepared ahead of time and kept ready, allowing for a swift assembly of a nutrient-dense breakfast bowl that meets your dog's dietary needs without eating into your precious morning time. The secret is to cook ingredients like chicken and sweet potatoes in large quantities during a relaxed weekend afternoon, making weekday mornings a time of easy routines instead of rushed chaos.

### Incorporating Variety

Variety, the spice of life, holds true for our canine friends, just as it does for us. Rotating ingredients within breakfast bowls not only prevents mealtime monotony but also ensures a broad spectrum of nutrients. Monday might feature a base of brown rice, rich in fiber, topped with scrambled eggs and diced apples for a crunch. On the other hand, on Wednesday, we could see a blend of quinoa, rich in protein and essential amino acids, with cooked ground turkey and kale. This rotation, much like changing the course of a walk from the park to the beach, keeps excitement alive, encouraging eager-ness and anticipation at mealtime.

**Balancing Macronutrients**

Creating a well-rounded breakfast bowl for your dog with proteins, fats, and carbohydrates plays together in perfect balance. Think of proteins as the cornerstone of the meal, essential for building and repairing muscles and tissues. These should be complemented by carbohydrates, which act as the fuel source for your dog's day, and fats, which are necessary for absorbing vitamins and providing a healthy shine to their coat. For example, a combination of salmon, rich in omega-3 fatty acids, for a glossy coat, sweet potatoes for a boost of energy, and green beans for fiber strikes an ideal balance. This careful mix of macronutrients is key to delivering a meal that not only satisfies but also supports your dog's energy levels, overall health, and well-being.

**Hydration Boost**

Morning meals offer a prime opportunity to boost your dog's daily water intake, especially for those who might not drink enough throughout the day. Incorporating hydrating ingredients like cucumber or watermelon into breakfast bowls, or even adding a splash of bone broth, can significantly contribute to your dog's hydration.

## 4.2 PROTEIN-PACKED DINNERS FOR OPTIMAL HEALTH

As day transitions into night, the act of preparing your dog's dinner becomes a meaningful gesture toward their health and vitality. Selecting the right protein sources is crucial, as they are the corner-stone of a diet that supports muscle repair, boosts energy levels, and fortifies the immune system.

Opt for lean meats, which are excellent sources of essential amino acids and provide substantial nutrition without high-fat content. Poultry, especially chicken breast, is another good source of lean protein, though it's essential to cook it properly to eliminate any risk of pathogens. Fish, rich in both protein and omega-3 fatty acids supports cognitive function and promotes a healthy coat. However, it's important to be cautious with certain types of fish that may have high levels of mercury, like raw salmon, which could contain parasites harmful to your dog.

Crafting these protein-rich dinners involves a thoughtful blend of ingredients, transforming simple components into nourishing meals. By combining proteins with fibrous vegetables and wholesome carbohydrates, these dinners satisfy hunger while also ensuring a steady release of energy. This approach helps maintain your dog's energy levels, preventing the ups and downs that can occur with less balanced meals. As the evening winds down, this nutritional harmony supports your dog's body through its overnight repair and growth processes, with proteins serving as the essential building blocks for recovery.

Portion control, often overlooked in the excitement of providing, has become a critical aspect of dinner preparation. The caloric and nutritional needs of a sprightly terrier differ vastly from those of a languid Great Dane; thus, tailoring portion sizes to fit the individual dog's size, breed, and activity level becomes imperative. This customization ensures that the fuel provided matches the expenditure and needs of the body, promoting optimal health without the risk of overfeeding or underfeeding. It is a delicate balance that requires observation and adjustment, as your dog's needs may evolve with age, health status, and seasonal changes in activity.

Occasionally, adding plant-based proteins like lentils or chickpeas can be beneficial for dogs who digest them well, adding not only a new taste but also valuable fiber and nutrients not found in meat. By rotating through different proteins, we avoid nutritional imbalances, ensuring no single nutrient overshadows another.

## 4.3 HEALTHY FATS AND OILS FOR COAT SHINE AND SKIN HEALTH

In the world of dog nutrition, fats and oils are crucial, not just for providing energy but also for contributing to the health and appearance of your dog's coat and skin. Omega-3 and Omega-6 fatty acids are key components that help maintain the luster of their coat and the vitality of their skin. Achieving the right balance of these fats is essential. It ensures that your pet's fur remains soft and glossy to the touch, while their skin stays hydrated and irritation-free.

The search for essential nutrients introduces us to a variety of sources, each abundant in the fatty acids vital for your dog's health. Fish oils, a rich source of Omega-3s, are key for reducing inflammation and promoting cell health. Alternatively, flaxseed provides a plant-based source of these beneficial oils, showcasing nature's ability to cater to our pets' dietary needs. Nuts like almonds are also valuable, offering Omega-6 fatty acids crucial for maintaining dietary balance. Together, these diverse sources allow for a well-rounded approach to incorporating essential fats into your dog's diet, ensuring a healthy coat and resilient skin.

The key is to integrate these oils smoothly into the dog's diet, such as by adding a drizzle of fish oil over softly cooked meats or a sprinkle of ground flaxseed over mashed vegetables. This approach ensures that each meal is not only a source of nourishment but also a pleasure for your dog to eat. The oils blend effortlessly into the dishes, enhancing without overpowering the meal's natural flavors. This thoughtful addition aims to respect your dog's taste preferences while providing the nutritional benefits needed for a healthy coat and skin.

However, while enriching your dog's diet with these vital fats and oils, it's crucial to remember that moderation is key. Overseeing the fat content in your dog's meals is a form of care, ensuring their diet maintains a healthy equilibrium. The right balance is evident not only in a shiny coat and soft skin, but also in your dog's vitality and agility. Too much fat, especially the saturated kind, can lead to unwanted weight gain and associated health issues, scenarios we aim to sidestep. Therefore, we mindfully measure the addition of fats and oils to their diet, aiming to provide the perfect amount of nourishment without the risk of overindulgence.

## 4.4 CARB CHOICES: SAFE VEGETABLES AND FRUITS

In preparing meals for our dogs, selecting the right carbohydrates is just as crucial as picking the right proteins and fats. It's not just about filling their bowls, but choosing vegetables and fruits that are safe, energizing, and supportive of their digestive health.

**Safe and Healthy Options**

When it comes to vegetables, the array that nature offers is both rich and diverse, each with its own unique profile of vitamins, minerals, and fiber. Green beans, for instance, stand out as a crunchy treat that can be served raw or lightly steamed, offering a low-calorie option rich in fiber. Carrots, with their sweet crunch, serve not only as a source of beta-carotene but also as a dental aid that promotes oral health through the natural action of chewing. Pumpkin, when cooked and pureed, becomes a gentle remedy for digestive ailments because of its fiber content, which supports bowel regularity. Broccoli, though nutritious, demands moderation due to its potential to cause gas, a reminder of the delicate balance required in meal composition.

Fruits, with their burst of sweetness, offer variety and are a natural source of vitamins and antioxidants. Apples, seeds removed, provide a refreshing crunch full of fiber and vitamin C, making them an ideal occasional snack. Blueberries, small yet mighty, pack a powerful punch of antioxidants, supporting cellular health and cognitive function. Watermelon, with its high water content, offers a hydrating treat, particularly refreshing during the warmer months, though its sugar content necessitates moderation.

When incorporating vegetables and fruits into your dog's meals, it's crucial to focus not just on choosing the right items but also on how they are prepared. Lightly steaming vegetables can enhance their digestibility while preserving their nutritional content, making them more suitable for your dog's digestive system. Fruits should be thoroughly washed and cut into appropriate sizes to prevent choking hazards, and they should always be served without any seeds or pits to ensure they deliver their health benefits safely.

**Carbs for Energy**

The role of carbohydrates in providing essential energy for active dogs is undeniable. The inclusion of such ingredients as sweet potatoes and butternut squash, both complex carbohydrates, ensures a steady release of energy, sustaining your dog's activity levels throughout the day. Unlike simple carbohydrates, which can cause spikes in blood sugar, these complex options offer sustained fuel, supporting everything from daily walks to playful endeavors without the risk of a rapid decline in energy.

**Fiber for Digestion**

Fiber, the unsung hero of digestive health, finds its champions in the vegetable and fruit selections of a dog's meal. Beyond its role in regulating bowel movements, fiber supports a healthy gut microbiome, fostering a community of beneficial bacteria that aid in digestion and nutrient absorption. The inclusion of fibrous vegetables such as peas and fruits like raspberries in a dog's diet acts as a preventive measure against constipation and diarrhea, promoting overall gastrointestinal health. This focus on fiber underscores the interconnectedness of diet and digestion, reminding us that what we choose to feed our dogs extends its influence far beyond the bowl.

## 4.5 SPECIAL NEEDS DIETS: LOW-CALORIE MEALS FOR WEIGHT MANAGEMENT

As we lovingly care for our dogs, it's crucial to recognize how easily excess weight can creep up on them, diminishing their health and energy. This widespread issue calls for our careful attention, emphasizing the need for a balanced diet that controls calories without skimping on nutrition.

### Identifying Overweight Dogs

The owner's observant eyes are the first crucial step in managing your dog's weight. Skillfully detecting the nuances between a fit body and one carrying extra weight is key. This evaluation goes beyond mere looks, focusing on whether you can easily feel your dog's ribs, spot a defined waist from above, and notice a distinct abdominal tuck. If these indicators are missing or less pronounced, it signals the need for a careful adjustment in their diet, focusing on carefully crafted meals that help restore a healthy balance.

### Calorie Control

The key to creating fulfilling, low-calorie meals lies in choosing the right ingredients that pack a flavor punch without the calorie overload. Opting for lean proteins ensures a rich, satisfying base without unnecessary fat. Vegetables, with their high volume and fiber content, fill up your dog without piling on the calories.

Adding a careful amount of whole grains can offer a steady energy supply, avoiding the calorie excess that leads to weight gain. This thoughtful approach to meal preparation ensures each bite is nutrient-dense, avoiding excess while maintaining satisfaction.

**Exercise Integration**

The relationship between a healthy diet and regular physical activity is crucial for managing your dog's weight effectively. Understanding that the calories your dog burns should outnumber those they consume highlights the need for exercise that is both enjoyable and suited to your dog's unique preferences and abilities. Incorporating a variety of activities, such as energizing walks and playful games that spark their curiosity, makes the journey toward weight loss engaging rather than tedious. This strategy transforms exercise into a valued part of your dog's routine, amplifying the positive impact of the dietary changes you've made.

**Regular Monitoring**

Weight management is a continuous process, not marked by occasional checks but by the regularity of weigh-ins. These check-ups serve as key milestones, offering valuable insights for any necessary dietary tweaks to meet your dog's changing needs. The scale provides a clear indicator of the progress made through your dietary and exercise efforts, either confirming the effectiveness of your current approach or signaling the need for adjustments. This cycle of observation and modification reflects the ever-changing nature of health, emphasizing that it's shaped day by day through our decisions.

## 4.6 HYDRATING HOMEMADE BROTHS AND SOUPS

Incorporating broths and soups into your dog's diet goes beyond simple nourishment, offering a holistic approach to their well-being. These liquid meals, often seen as mere comfort foods, are actually packed with a multitude of benefits that surpass just hydration. By adding broths and soups to your pet's diet, you're providing them with essential nutrients in a highly digestible and enjoyable form. The slow simmering of bones, vegetables, and herbs not only extracts their core nutrients into a flavorful liquid, but it also connects to traditional practices of making every ingredient count. This method ensures no part of the meal goes to waste while also delivering a rich source of vitamins, minerals, and hydration to your dog.

The advantages of adding broths and soups to your dog's diet are vast. These liquid meals are crucial for hydration, particularly for dogs that tend to drink less water. They are rich sources of essential minerals such as calcium, phosphorus, magnesium, and potassium, which are extracted from bones and vegetables through slow cooking. Additionally, they are packed with vitamins and amino acids critical for joint health and digestive support. Broths and soups are especially beneficial for recuperating dogs or those on a soft diet, providing a comforting and easily digestible meal that aids in healing and recovery.

A simple recipe might begin with a base of chicken, beef, or fish bones, selected for their richness in collagen, which supports joint health and skin elasticity. To this foundation, a variety of vegetables such as carrots, celery, and parsley can be added, not only for their nutrient content but also for the depth of flavor they bring to the broth. A slow simmer is key because it allows for the gradual release of nutrients into the broth, creating a nutrient-dense liquid that can be served on its own or as a base for more complex soups.

Broths and soups are used to enhance dry meals or entice picky eaters, adding a layer of versatility to these liquid nourishments. A splash of broth over kibble transforms an ordinary meal into a savory, moist feast, enticing even the most reluctant eater. For dogs that require enticement due to illness or loss of appetite, the aroma and flavor of a warm soup can be an irresistible call to dine, providing not only hydration and nourishment but also comfort and encouragement to eat.

Preparing large batches of broth and storing them for convenience ensures that this liquid gold is always on hand to enrich your dog's diet. Once cooled, broth can be portioned into ice cube trays or freezer-safe containers, creating single servings that can be easily thawed and added to meals. This method of storage not only capitalizes on the efficiency of batch cooking but also ensures that the broth retains its nutritional value, ready to be deployed at a moment's notice to elevate a meal or offer a hydrating treat.

In closing, the essence of this chapter reaches beyond the recipes and techniques to touch on the heart of what it means to care for our canine companions. It's a reminder that every meal offers the chance to provide more than just nutrition; it's an opportunity to enrich their lives in meaningful ways.

## HEALTHY HOMEMADE CHICKEN RECIPES FOR DOGS

## SUNDANCE'S CHICKEN AND RICE ROUNDUP

Let all meals cool before serving. Do not serve hot food to your dog.

**Ingredients:**

- 2 cups chicken breast, boiled and shredded
- 1 cup brown rice
- 1/2 cup peas
- 1 carrot, diced
- 3 cups chicken broth (no onion or garlic)

**Preparation:**

1. **Cook the chicken:** Boil the chicken breast until fully cooked, then shred.
2. **Cook the rice:** In a separate pot, cook the brown rice in chicken broth until tender.
3. **Steam the vegetables:** Steam the carrots and peas until soft.
4. **Combine:** Mix the cooked chicken, rice, carrots, and peas together.

**Cooking Time:** 50 minutes

**Nutrition (per cup):**

- Calories: 220
- Protein: 18g
- Fat: 6g
- Vitamins: A, B-complex
- Minerals: zinc, iron

**Serving Sizes:**

- Small dogs: 1/2 cup
- Medium dogs: 1 cup
- Large dogs: 1 1/2 cups

## CHARLIE'S CHICKEN AND PUMPKIN STEW

**Ingredients:**

- 2 cups chicken breast, boiled and shredded
- 1 cup canned pumpkin (not pie filling)
- 1/2 cup green beans, chopped
- 1 apple, cored and chopped
- 2 cups water

**Preparation:**

1. **Cook the chicken:** Boil the chicken breast until fully cooked, then shred.
2. **Combine all ingredients:** In a large pot, mix the shredded chicken, pumpkin, green beans, and apple with water.
3. **Cook:** Simmer for about 20 minutes until the apple is soft.

**Cooking Time:** 45 minutes

**Nutrition (per cup):**

- Calories: 180
- Protein: 16g
- Fat: 4g
- Fiber: 3g
- Vitamins: A, C, E

**Serving Sizes:**

- Small dogs: 1/2 cup
- Medium dogs: 3/4 cup
- Large dogs: 1 1/4 cups

## BELLA'S CHICKEN AND SWEET POTATO MASH

**Ingredients:**

- 2 cups chicken breast, boiled and shredded
- 1 large sweet potato, peeled, boiled, and mashed
- 1/2 cup cooked quinoa
- 1 tablespoon olive oil
- 2 cups chicken broth

**Preparation:**

1. **Prepare the chicken:** Boil the chicken breast until fully cooked, then shred.
2. **Cook the sweet potato:** Peel and cube the sweet potato, boil until tender, drain, and mash.
3. **Cook the quinoa:** Cook the quinoa according to package instructions.
4. **Combine:** In a large pot, mix the shredded chicken, mashed sweet potato, and cooked quinoa with chicken broth. Cook over low heat to integrate all the ingredients.

**Cooking Time:** 60 minutes

**Nutrition (per cup):**

- Calories: 240
- Protein: 20g

- Fat: 8g
- Fiber: 3g
- Vitamins: A, B6, C
- Minerals: Calcium, magnesium, iron

**Serving Sizes:**

- Small dogs: 1/2 cup
- Medium dogs: 1 cup
- Large dogs: 1 1/2 cups

## LUCY'S CHICKEN VEGGIE MASH

**Ingredients:**

- 2 cups chicken breast, boiled and shredded
- 1 cup cauliflower, chopped
- 1/2 cup broccoli, chopped
- 1/2 cup carrots, chopped
- 2 tablespoons coconut oil
- 2 cups water

**Preparation:**

1. **Cook the chicken:** Boil the chicken until fully cooked, then shred.
2. **Steam vegetables:** Steam the cauliflower, broccoli, and carrots until soft.
3. **Blend:** In a blender, puree the steamed vegetables with coconut oil and some water until smooth.
4. **Combine:** Mix the vegetable puree with shredded chicken and warm through.

**Cooking Time:** 50 minutes

**Nutrition (per cup):**

- Calories: 210
- Protein: 19g
- Fat: 10g
- Vitamins: K, C
- Minerals: Potassium

**Serving Sizes:**

- Small dogs: 1/2 cup
- Medium dogs: 1 cup
- Large dogs: 1 1/2 cups

## MAX'S CHICKEN AND OATS SURPRISE

**Ingredients:**

- 2 cups chicken breast, boiled and chopped
- 1 cup rolled oats, cooked
- 1/2 cup blueberries
- 1 tablespoon flaxseed oil
- 2 cups water

**Preparation:**

1. **Cook the chicken:** Boil the chicken until fully cooked, then chop.
2. **Cook the oats:** In a pot, cook the oats in water until soft.
3. **Combine:** In a large bowl, mix the cooked chicken, cooked oats, blueberries, and flaxseed oil.

**Cooking Time:** 40 minutes

**Nutrition (per cup):**

- Calories: 230
- Protein: 17g
- Fat: 8g
- Fiber: 2g
- Vitamins: B-complex, E

**Serving Sizes:**

- Small dogs: 1/2 cup
- Medium dogs: 3/4 cup
- Large dogs: 1 1/4 cups

## RUSTY'S CHICKEN AND LENTILS DELIGHT

**Ingredients:**

- 2 cups chicken breast, boiled and shredded
- 1 cup lentils, cooked
- 1 carrot, diced
- 1/2 cup spinach, chopped
- 2 tablespoons olive oil
- 2 cups water

**Preparation:**

1. **Prepare the chicken:** Boil the chicken breast until fully cooked, then shred.
2. **Cook lentils:** Cook lentils according to package instructions until tender.
3. **Steam the spinach and carrot:** In a steamer, steam the diced carrot and spinach until soft.

4. **Combine:** In a large pot, mix the shredded chicken, cooked lentils, steamed vegetables, and olive oil. Heat through to combine the flavors.

**Cooking Time:** 50 minutes

**Nutrition (per cup):**

- Calories: 220
- Protein: 20g
- Fat: 9g
- Fiber: 4g
- Vitamins: A, C, Iron

**Serving Sizes:**

- Small dogs: 1/2 cup
- Medium dogs: 1 cup
- Large dogs: 1 1/2 cups

## LUNA'S CHICKEN PEA PILAF

**Ingredients:**

- 2 cups chicken breast, boiled and shredded
- 1 cup brown rice, cooked
- 1/2 cup peas, cooked
- 1 tablespoon sunflower oil
- 2 cups chicken broth

**Preparation:**

1. **Cook the chicken:** Boil the chicken breast until fully cooked, then shred.

2. **Cook the rice:** Cook brown rice in chicken broth until tender.
3. **Cook the peas:** Boil the peas until tender.
4. **Combine:** In a large pot, mix the shredded chicken, cooked rice, peas, and sunflower oil. Heat through to integrate flavors.

**Cooking Time:** 60 minutes

**Nutrition (per cup):**

- Calories: 210
- Protein: 18g
- Fat: 7g
- Fiber: 2g
- Vitamins: B-complex, E

**Serving Sizes:**

- Small dogs: 1/2 cup
- Medium dogs: 1 cup
- Large dogs: 1 1/2 cups

## BLACKIES CHICKEN AND BARLEY SOUP

**Ingredients:**

- 2 cups chicken breast, boiled and shredded
- 1 cup barley, cooked
- 1/2 cup carrots, diced
- 1 celery stalk, chopped
- 3 cups chicken broth

**Preparation:**

1. **Prepare the chicken:** Boil the chicken breast until fully cooked, then shred.
2. **Cook the barley:** Cook the barley in chicken broth until tender.
3. **Cook vegetables:** Steam the diced carrots and chopped celery until soft.
4. **Combine:** In a large pot, mix the shredded chicken, cooked barley, steamed vegetables, and remaining chicken broth. Simmer for 10 minutes to blend the flavors.

**Cooking Time:** 70 minutes

**Nutrition (per cup):**

- Calories: 190
- Protein: 18g
- Fat: 4g
- Fiber: 3g
- Vitamins: A, C

**Serving Sizes:**

- Small dogs: 1/2 cup
- Medium dogs: 3/4 cup
- Large dogs: 1 1/4 cups

## AUGIE'S CHICKEN APPLE CRUNCH

**Ingredients:**

- 2 cups chicken breast, boiled and shredded
- 1 apple, cored and chopped

- 1/2 cup cooked brown rice
- 1 tablespoon coconut oil
- 2 cups water

**Preparation:**

1. **Cook the chicken:** Boil the chicken breast until fully cooked, then shred.
2. **Cook the apple:** In a small pot, add chopped apple and a bit of water, and cook until soft.
3. **Combine:** In a large bowl, mix the shredded chicken, cooked apple, cooked brown rice, and coconut oil.

**Cooking Time:** 45 minutes

**Nutrition (per cup):**

- Calories: 200
- Protein: 16g
- Fat: 7g
- Fiber: 2g
- Vitamins: C, E

**Serving Sizes:**

- Small dogs: 1/2 cup
- Medium dogs: 3/4 cup
- Large dogs: 1 1/4 cups

## SADIE'S CHICKEN AND VEGGIE KIBBLE MIX

**Ingredients:**

- 2 cups chicken breast, boiled and shredded

- 1 cup cooked quinoa
- 1/2 cup carrots, diced
- 1/2 cup zucchini, diced
- 2 tablespoons olive oil
- 2 cups water

**Preparation:**

1. **Prepare the chicken:** Boil the chicken breast until fully cooked, then shred.
2. **Cook the quinoa:** Cook quinoa according to package instructions until fluffy.
3. **Steam vegetables:** Steam the diced carrots and zucchini until tender.
4. **Combine:** In a large bowl, mix the shredded chicken, cooked quinoa, steamed vegetables, and olive oil. Serve warm or cooled.

**Cooking Time:** 60 minutes

**Nutrition (per cup):**

- Calories: 210
- Protein: 19g
- Fat: 10g
- Fiber: 2g
- Vitamins: A, C, E

**Serving Sizes:**

- Small dogs: 1/2 cup
- Medium dogs: 1 cup
- Large dogs: 1 1/2 cups

Each recipe provides a nutritious, balanced meal for your dog, designed to be both healthy and budget-friendly. Adjust portions based on your dog's size, age, and activity level.

## HEALTHY HOMEMADE BEEF RECIPES FOR DOGS

## ALDO'S BEEF AND RICE CASSEROLE

Let all meals cool before serving. Do not serve hot food to your dog.

**Ingredients:**

- 2 cups beef, boiled and shredded
- 1 cup white rice, cooked
- 1/2 cup mixed vegetables (carrots, peas, and corn), boiled
- 2 tablespoons olive oil
- 2 cups beef broth

**Preparation:**

1. **Cook the beef:** Boil the beef until fully cooked, then shred.
2. **Cook the rice:** Cook white rice in beef broth until fluffy.
3. **Boil the vegetables:** Boil the mixed vegetables until soft.
4. **Combine:** In a large pot, mix the shredded beef, cooked rice, cooked vegetables, and olive oil. Heat through to integrate flavors.

**Cooking Time:** 60 minutes

**Nutrition (per cup):**

- Calories: 225
- Protein: 20g
- Fat: 10g
- Fiber: 2g
- Vitamins: A, B-complex

**Serving Sizes:**

- Small dogs: 1/2 cup
- Medium dogs: 1 cup
- Large dogs: 1 1/2 cups

## NIKI'S HEARTY BEEF STEW

**Ingredients:**

- 2 cups beef, boiled and shredded
- 1 potato, diced and boiled
- 1/2 cup chopped celery
- 1 carrot, diced
- 3 cups beef broth

**Preparation:**

1. **Prepare the beef:** Boil the beef until fully cooked, then shred.
2. **Boil the potato and vegetables:** Boil the diced potato, celery, and carrot until tender.
3. **Combine:** In a large pot, mix the shredded beef, boiled

vegetables, and beef broth. Simmer for 10 minutes to blend flavors.

**Cooking Time:** 50 minutes

**Nutrition (per cup):**

- Calories: 210
- Protein: 18g
- Fat: 8g
- Fiber: 3g
- Vitamins: A, C, B-complex

**Serving Sizes:**

- Small dogs: 1/2 cup
- Medium dogs: 3/4 cup
- Large dogs: 1 1/4 cups

## BUD'S BEEFY BARLEY BOWL

**Ingredients:**

- 2 cups beef, boiled and shredded
- 1 cup barley, cooked
- 1/2 cup spinach, chopped and steamed
- 2 tablespoons canola oil
- 2 cups beef broth

**Preparation:**

1. **Cook the beef:** Boil the beef until fully cooked, then shred it.
2. **Cook the barley:** Cook the barley in water until tender.

3. **Steam the spinach:** Steam the chopped spinach until wilted.
4. **Combine:** In a large pot, mix the shredded beef, cooked barley, steamed spinach, canola oil, and beef broth. Warm through to combine.

**Cooking Time:** 70 minutes

**Nutrition (per cup):**

- Calories: 230
- Protein: 21g
- Fat: 12g
- Fiber: 3g
- Vitamins: A, C, Iron

**Serving Sizes:**

- Small dogs: 1/2 cup
- Medium dogs: 1 cup
- Large dogs: 1 1/2 cups

## SEAMUS'S BEEFY MASH

**Ingredients:**

- 2 cups beef, boiled and shredded
- 1 cup mashed potatoes
- 1/2 cup carrots, steamed and mashed
- 1 tablespoon coconut oil
- 2 cups water

**Preparation:**

1. **Prepare the beef:** Boil the beef until fully cooked, then shred.
2. **Prepare the mash:** Mash the boiled potatoes and steamed carrots together with coconut oil.
3. **Combine:** Mix the shredded beef with the vegetable mash and add water to adjust consistency.

**Cooking Time:** 45 minutes

**Nutrition (per cup):**

- Calories: 240
- Protein: 20g
- Fat: 14g
- Fiber: 3g
- Vitamins: A, C

**Serving Sizes:**

- Small dogs: 1/2 cup
- Medium dogs: 3/4 cup
- Large dogs: 1 1/4 cups

## DAKOTA'S NUTRITIOUS BEEF AND VEGGIE MIX

**Ingredients:**

- 2 cups beef, boiled and shredded
- 1/2 cup quinoa, cooked
- 1/2 cup pumpkin, steamed and mashed
- 1/4 cup green beans, chopped and steamed
- 1 tablespoon olive oil

- 2 cups water

**Preparation:**

1. **Cook the beef:** Boil the beef until fully cooked, then shred.
2. **Cook quinoa:** Cook quinoa according to package instructions.
3. **Prepare vegetables:** Steam the pumpkin and green beans, then mash the pumpkin.
4. **Combine:** In a large pot, mix the shredded beef, cooked quinoa, mashed pumpkin, steamed green beans, olive oil, and water. Heat through to combine.

**Cooking Time:** 60 minutes

**Nutrition (per cup):**

- Calories: 220
- Protein: 21g
- Fat: 10g
- Fiber: 4g
- Vitamins: A, C, E

**Serving Sizes:**

- Small dogs: 1/2 cup
- Medium dogs: 1 cup
- Large dogs: 1 1/2 cups

## BAILEY'S BEEF, RICE, AND PEA PATTIES

**Ingredients:**

- 2 cups beef, boiled and finely chopped

- 1 cup cooked white rice
- 1/2 cup peas, mashed
- 1 egg, beaten
- 2 tablespoons sunflower oil

**Preparation:**

1. **Prepare the beef:** Boil the beef until fully cooked, then finely chop.
2. **Mix ingredients:** In a bowl, mix the chopped beef, cooked rice, mashed peas, and beaten egg to form a consistent mixture.
3. **Form patties:** Shape the mixture into small patties.
4. **Cook patties:** In a pan, heat the sunflower oil and cook the patties until golden brown on both sides.

**Cooking Time:** 30 minutes

**Nutrition (per patty):**

- Calories: 150
- Protein: 14g
- Fat: 8g
- Fiber: 1g
- Vitamins: B-complex

**Serving Sizes:**

- Small dogs: 1 patty
- Medium dogs: 2 patties
- Large dogs: 3 patties

## MOLLY'S BEEF AND ZUCCHINI STIR-FRY

**Ingredients:**

- 2 cups beef, boiled and sliced
- 1 cup zucchini, sliced
- 1/2 cup carrots, sliced
- 1 tablespoon sesame oil
- 1 teaspoon turmeric

**Preparation:**

1. **Cook the beef:** Boil the beef until fully cooked, then slice.
2. **Stir-fry:** In a pan, heat the sesame oil and sauté the sliced beef, zucchini, and carrots with turmeric until the vegetables are tender.

**Cooking Time:** 20 minutes

**Nutrition (per cup):**

- Calories: 200
- Protein: 18g
- Fat: 12g
- Fiber: 2g
- Vitamins: C, K

**Serving Sizes:**

- Small dogs: 1/2 cup
- Medium dogs: 3/4 cup
- Large dogs: 1 cup

# DAISY'S GROUND BEEF AND POTATO GRATIN

**Ingredients:**

- 2 cups ground beef, cooked
- 1 cup potatoes, sliced and boiled
- 1/2 cup low-fat cheese, grated
- 1/4 cup milk
- 1 tablespoon olive oil

**Preparation:**

1. **Cook the beef:** Cook the ground beef in a pan until browned.
2. **Layer and bake:** In a baking dish, layer the cooked beef, and sliced potatoes, and sprinkle it with cheese. Pour milk over the top and drizzle with olive oil. Bake in a preheated oven at 350°F for 20 minutes.

**Cooking Time:** 45 minutes

**Nutrition (per cup):**

- Calories: 230
- Protein: 20g
- Fat: 14g
- Calcium: High
- Vitamins: B12

**Serving Sizes:**

- Small dogs: 1/2 cup
- Medium dogs: 3/4 cup
- Large dogs: 1 cup

## COCO'S SLOW-COOKED BEEF AND APPLE DELIGHT

**Ingredients:**

- 2 cups beef, cubed
- 1 apple, peeled and chopped
- 1/2 cup oats
- 1 teaspoon cinnamon
- 2 cups water.

**Preparation:**

1. **Prepare ingredients:** Place the beef cubes, chopped apple, oats, and cinnamon in a slow cooker.
2. **Slow cook:** Cover with water and cook on low for 6 hours.

**Cooking Time:** 6 hours

**Nutrition (per cup):**

- Calories: 180
- Protein: 16g
- Fat: 8g
- Fiber: 3g
- Vitamins: C, B-complex

**Serving Sizes:**

- Small dogs: 1/2 cup
- Medium dogs: 3/4 cup
- Large dogs: 1 cup

# GUINNESS'S BEEF AND EGG BREAKFAST SCRAMBLE

**Ingredients:**

- 2 cups beef, boiled and chopped
- 2 eggs, beaten
- 1/2 cup spinach, chopped
- 1 tablespoon butter.

**Preparation:**

1. **Cook the beef:** Boil the beef until fully cooked, then chop.
2. **Scramble:** Melt the butter and add the chopped beef and spinach in a pan. Pour in the beaten eggs and scramble until the eggs are set.

**Cooking Time:** 15 minutes

**Nutrition (per serving):**

- Calories: 250
- Protein: 22g
- Fat: 16g
- Fiber: 1g
- Vitamins: A, D, Iron

**Serving Sizes:**

- Small dogs: 1/2 cup
- Medium dogs: 3/4 cup
- Large dogs: 1 cup

The recipes provide a variety of tasty and nutritious options for your dog, each designed to be easy to prepare and cost-effective for regular feeding. Adjust serving sizes based on your dog's size, age, and activity level to meet their dietary needs.

## HEALTHY PROTEIN OPTIONS FOR DOGS

1. **Chicken**: A great source of protein, vitamins, and minerals. Ensure it's cooked thoroughly and bones are removed to prevent choking or internal injuries.
2. **Turkey**: A protein source. Just like chicken, make sure it's cooked and free from bones and excessive fat. Avoid seasoned preparations that might contain harmful spices.
3. **Beef**: Rich in protein, iron, and several important vitamins. It should be cooked without harmful seasonings or sauces. Fatty cuts should be limited to avoid pancreatitis.
4. **Lamb**: It is often used as an alternative protein source for dogs that may have allergies to beef or chicken. It should be cooked and served plain.
5. **Pork**: Safe for dogs, but it should be cooked thoroughly without seasonings. Pork is also richer and fattier than other meats, so it should be given in moderation.
6. **Fish**: Many types of fish, including salmon, sardines, and cod, are excellent sources of protein and omega-3 fatty acids. Fish should be cooked and deboned. Avoid high-mercury fish like tuna and swordfish.
7. **Bison**: Lean and rich in protein, bison is a good alternative for dogs that may be allergic to more common meats. It should be cooked without added spices or sauces.
8. **Venison**: Another great alternative protein source, especially for dogs with sensitivities or allergies. It should be cooked and free from seasonings.

9. **Rabbit**: Lean and nutritious, suitable for dogs, especially those with dietary sensitivities. It should be cooked plain.

10. **Duck**: Rich in iron and a good protein source, duck can be a good choice for an alternative protein. It should be cooked and served without the skin to reduce fat content.

**When feeding your dog meat, it's important to:**

- **Cook all meat thoroughly** to kill potentially harmful bacteria.
- **Remove all bones**, particularly from poultry, as they can splinter and cause digestive tract injuries.
- **Avoid seasoning and sauces**, as many seasonings are toxic to dogs (e.g., onion, garlic).
- **Moderate fat content**, especially for dogs prone to pancreatitis.

Introduce new meats gradually into your dog's diet to monitor for any adverse reactions or allergies. Consulting with a veterinarian about your dog's diet is also advisable to ensure their specific dietary needs are met appropriately.

## HEALTHY HOMEMADE FISH RECIPES FOR DOGS

## DUKE'S SIMPLE FISH AND RICE

Do not serve hot food to your dog, allow it to cool down before serving.

**Ingredients:**

- 2 cups white fish (e.g., cod or tilapia), cooked and flaked
- 1 cup brown rice, cooked
- 1/2 cup peas, boiled
- 2 tablespoons olive oil
- 2 cups water

**Preparation:**

1. **Cook the fish:** Boil or steam the fish until fully cooked, then flake with a fork.
2. **Cook the rice:** Cook brown rice in water until fluffy.
3. **Boil the peas:** Boil the peas until soft.
4. **Combine:** In a large bowl, mix the flaked fish, cooked rice, peas, and olive oil.

**Cooking Time:** 50 minutes

**Nutrition (per cup):**

- Calories: 220
- Protein: 20g
- Fat: 8g
- Fiber: 2g
- Omega-3 fatty acids

**Serving Sizes:**

- Small dogs: 1/2 cup

- Medium dogs: 1 cup
- Large dogs: 1 1/2 cups

## HENRY'S FISH AND SWEET POTATO STEW

**Ingredients:**

- 2 cups salmon, boiled and shredded
- 1 large sweet potato, peeled, boiled, and mashed
- 1/2 cup carrots, boiled and mashed
- 2 tablespoons coconut oil
- 2 cups water.

**Preparation:**

1. **Cook the salmon:** Boil the salmon until fully cooked, then shred.
2. **Cook and mash the sweet potato and carrots:** Boil the sweet potato and carrots until tender, then mash.
3. **Combine:** In a large pot, mix the shredded salmon, mashed sweet potato, mashed carrots, coconut oil, and water. Heat through to combine the mixture.

**Cooking Time:** 60 minutes

**Nutrition (per cup):**

- Calories: 250
- Protein: 22g
- Fat: 12g
- Fiber: 3g
- Vitamins: A, C

**Serving Sizes:**

- Small dogs: 1/2 cup
- Medium dogs: 1 cup
- Large dogs: 1 1/2 cups

## STELLA'S SALMON AND RICE CASSEROLE

**Ingredients:**

- 2 cups salmon, canned in water, drained
- 1 cup white rice, cooked
- 1/2 cup green beans, chopped and steamed
- 1 tablespoon olive oil
- 2 cups fish broth.

**Preparation:**

1. **Prepare the salmon:** Drain the canned salmon.
2. **Cook the rice:** Cook white rice in fish broth until tender.
3. **Steam the green beans:** Steam the chopped green beans until tender.
4. **Combine:** In a large pot, mix the salmon, cooked rice, green beans, and olive oil. Heat through to integrate flavors.

**Cooking Time:** 40 minutes

**Nutrition (per cup):**

- Calories: 210
- Protein: 18g
- Fat: 8g
- Fiber: 1g
- Omega-3 fatty acids.

**Serving Sizes:**

- Small dogs: 1/2 cup
- Medium dogs: 1 cup
- Large dogs: 1 1/2 cups.

## ELLIE'S FISH VEGETABLE MEDLEY

**Ingredients:**

- 2 cups white fish, cooked and flaked
- 1/2 cup broccoli, steamed and chopped
- 1/2 cup zucchini, steamed and chopped
- 2 tablespoons flaxseed oil
- 2 cups water.

**Preparation:**

1. **Cook the fish:** Boil or steam the fish until fully cooked, then flake.
2. **Steam the vegetables:** Steam broccoli and zucchini until tender.
3. **Combine:** In a large bowl, mix the flaked fish, steamed vegetables, flaxseed oil, and water.

**Cooking Time:** 40 minutes

**Nutrition (per cup):**

- Calories: 200
- Protein: 18g
- Fat: 10g
- Fiber: 2g
- Vitamins: C, K

**Serving Sizes:**

- Small dogs: 1/2 cup
- Medium dogs: 1 cup
- Large dogs: 1 1/2 cups

## TUCKER'S FISH AND EGG SCRAMBLE

**Ingredients:**

- 2 cups white fish, cooked and flaked
- 2 eggs, beaten
- 1/2 cup spinach, chopped
- 1 tablespoon butter
- 1/4 teaspoon turmeric

**Preparation:**

1. **Cook the fish:** Boil or steam the fish until fully cooked, then flake.
2. **Scramble the eggs:** In a pan, melt the butter, add turmeric, and then add the eggs and chopped spinach. Cook until the eggs are set.
3. **Combine:** Mix the flaked fish into the scrambled eggs.

**Cooking Time:** 20 minutes

**Nutrition (per serving):**

- Calories: 250
- Protein: 24g
- Fat: 14g
- Fiber: 1g
- Omega-3 fatty acids

**Serving Sizes:**

- Small dogs: 1/2 cup
- Medium dogs: 3/4 cup
- Large dogs: 1 cup

## BEAR'S SARDINE AND POTATO DINNER

**Ingredients:**

- 2 cups sardines, canned in water, drained
- 1 potato, boiled and mashed
- 1/2 cup carrots, steamed and mashed
- 1 tablespoon olive oil

**Preparation:**

1. **Prepare the sardines:** Drain the canned sardines.
2. **Cook and mash the potato and carrots:** Boil the potato and steam the carrots, then mash both.
3. **Combine:** In a large bowl, mix the sardines, mashed potato, mashed carrots, and olive oil.

**Cooking Time:** 40 minutes

**Nutrition (per cup):**

- Calories: 230
- Protein: 20g
- Fat: 12g
- Fiber: 2g
- Omega-3 fatty acids.

**Serving Sizes:**

- Small dogs: 1/2 cup
- Medium dogs: 1 cup
- Large dogs: 1 1/2 cups.

## NOLA'S SALMON AND PEA PUREE

**Ingredients:**

- 2 cups salmon, boiled and flaked
- 1/2 cup peas, boiled and pureed
- 1 tablespoon coconut oil
- 2 cups water.

**Preparation:**

1. **Cook the salmon:** Boil the salmon until fully cooked, then flake.
2. **Puree the peas:** Boil the peas until soft, then puree.
3. **Combine:** In a large pot, mix the flaked salmon, pea puree, coconut oil, and water. Heat through to combine.

**Cooking Time:** 35 minutes

**Nutrition (per cup):**

- Calories: 220
- Protein: 22g
- Fat: 12g
- Fiber: 2g
- Omega-3 fatty acids

**Serving Sizes:**

- Small dogs: 1/2 cup
- Medium dogs: 1 cup
- Large dogs: 1 1/2 cups.

## COOPER'S COD AND BARLEY SOUP

**Ingredients:**

- 2 cups cod, boiled and flaked
- 1 cup barley, cooked
- 1/2 cup chopped celery
- 2 cups fish broth.

**Preparation:**

1. **Cook the cod:** Boil the cod until fully cooked, then flake.
2. **Cook the barley:** Cook barley in fish broth until tender.
3. **Combine:** In a large pot, mix the flaked cod, cooked barley, and chopped celery with the remaining fish broth. Simmer it for 10 minutes to blend flavors.

**Cooking Time:** 60 minutes

**Nutrition (per cup):**

- Calories: 210
- Protein: 20g
- Fat: 6g
- Fiber: 3g
- Omega-3 fatty acids.

**Serving Sizes:**

- Small dogs: 1/2 cup
- Medium dogs: 3/4 cup
- Large dogs: 1 cup

## MAJOR'S HADDOCK AND RICE PILAF

**Ingredients:**

- 2 cups haddock, boiled and flaked
- 1 cup rice, cooked
- 1/2 cup peas, boiled
- 1 tablespoon sunflower oil
- 2 cups water.

**Preparation:**

1. **Cook the haddock:** Boil the haddock until fully cooked, then flake.
2. **Cook the rice:** Cook rice in water until fluffy.
3. **Boil the peas:** Boil the peas until tender.
4. **Combine:** In a large pot, mix the flaked haddock, cooked rice, boiled peas and sunflower oil. Heat through to integrate the flavors.

**Cooking Time:** 50 minutes

**Nutrition (per cup):**

- Calories: 215
- Protein: 19g
- Fat: 8g
- Fiber: 2g

- Omega-3 fatty acids.

**Serving Sizes:**

- Small dogs: 1/2 cup
- Medium dogs: 1 cup
- Large dogs: 1 1/2 cups.

## FINN'S TROUT AND VEGETABLE STIR-FRY

**Ingredients:**

- 2 cups trout, boiled and flaked
- 1/2 cup broccoli, steamed and chopped
- 1/2 cup carrots, steamed and chopped
- 2 tablespoons olive oil
- 1/4 teaspoon ginger, minced.

**Preparation:**

1. **Cook the trout:** Boil the trout until fully cooked, then flake.
2. **Steam the vegetables:** Steam the broccoli and carrots until tender.
3. **Stir-fry:** In a pan, heat the olive oil and sauté the flaked trout, steamed vegetables, and minced ginger until everything is well combined.

**Cooking Time:** 30 minutes

**Nutrition (per cup):**

- Calories: 210
- Protein: 22g
- Fat: 10g

- Fiber: 2g
- Omega-3 fatty acids.

**Serving Sizes:**

- Small dogs: 1/2 cup
- Medium dogs: 1 cup
- Large dogs: 1 1/2 cups.

These fish-based recipes provide an excellent source of omega-3 fatty acids and other essential nutrients, designed to be both delicious and healthy for your dog. Adjust the serving sizes according to your dog's size, age, and activity level to meet their specific dietary needs.

## HERE ARE SOME TYPES OF FISH THAT SHOULD BE AVOIDED IN DOG FOOD:

1. **Tilefish**: Known for their high levels of mercury, which can be harmful to dogs over time.
2. **Swordfish**: Very high in mercury, posing similar risks as tilefish.
3. **King Mackerel**: This type also contains high levels of mercury and should be avoided.
4. **Shark**: Like other high-mercury fish, shark is not suitable for dogs due to its potential toxicity.
5. **Albacore Tuna (White Tuna)**: Contains more mercury than light tuna and should be limited or avoided.
6. **Raw Salmon**: Fresh, raw salmon can contain parasites that cause "salmon poisoning disease," which is potentially fatal to dogs. Always cook salmon thoroughly before feeding it to your dog.

7. **Raw Pacific Herring**: This fish can also carry harmful parasites and should be thoroughly cooked before being fed to dogs.

8. **Smoked Seafood**: Often contains high levels of sodium and preservatives, which are not healthy for dogs.

9. **Fish with Small Bones**: Small, brittle bones, like those in sardines or smelt, can pose choking hazards or cause internal damage if not thoroughly processed.

When feeding fish to your dog, it's best to choose those that are low in mercury and other contaminants, such as salmon, flounder, or Arctic char, and ensure it is cooked well to kill any harmful pathogens. Always remove all bones, and consider consulting with a veterinarian to ensure that you're providing a diet that's safe and healthy for your specific pet.

## HEALTHY FRUITS FOR DOGS

### Apples

- **Nutrients**: Fiber, vitamin C, potassium
- **Benefits**: Good for digestion, helps clean teeth and freshens breath.

### Blueberries

- **Nutrients**: Antioxidants, vitamin C, vitamin K, fiber
- **Benefits**: Support heart health, brain function, and cancer prevention.

### Bananas

- **Nutrients**: Potassium, vitamin C, vitamin B6, fiber
- **Benefits**: Good for muscle and blood vessel function as well as overall energy.

### Watermelon

- **Nutrients**: Vitamins A, B6, C, and potassium
- **Benefits**: Hydrating due to high water content, low in calories.

### Strawberries

- **Nutrients**: Fiber, vitamin C, antioxidants
- **Benefits**: Helps strengthen the immune system and slow issues related to aging.

### Cranberries

- **Nutrients**: Fiber, vitamin C, manganese

- **Benefits**: Promote urinary tract health and reduce tartar and plaque buildup.

## Pears

- **Nutrients**: Fiber, vitamin C, copper
- **Benefits**: Good for colon health and antioxidative support.

## HEALTHY VEGETABLES FOR DOGS

## Carrots

- **Nutrients**: Beta-carotene (converted to vitamin A), fiber, vitamin K1, potassium
- **Benefits**: Good for the dog's teeth, skin, and coat health.

## Sweet Potatoes

- **Nutrients**: Beta-carotene, vitamins A, B6, and C, fiber
- **Benefits**: Supports immune function and digestive health.

## Pumpkin

- **Nutrients**: Fiber, vitamin A, antioxidants
- **Benefits**: Great for digestion and can help in managing diarrhea and constipation.

## Green Beans

- **Nutrients**: Iron, calcium, vitamins A, C, K, and B6, fiber
- **Benefits**: Low calorie and can help maintain a healthy weight.

## Spinach

- **Nutrients**: Iron, antioxidants, beta-carotene, fiber, vitamins A, B, C, K
- **Benefits**: Boosts the immune system, and protects against heart disease and cancer.

## Peas

- **Nutrients**: Vitamin K, manganese, vitamin C, fiber, thiamine
- **Benefits**: Supports metabolism and helps to maintain energy levels.

## Broccoli

- **Nutrients**: Fiber, vitamin C, vitamin K, iron, potassium

- **Benefits**: Supports detoxification processes in the body and promotes healthy skin.

## Zucchini

- **Nutrients**: Vitamins A, C, and K, potassium, fiber
- **Benefits**: Low calorie, helps in weight management, and promotes cardiovascular health.

## Kale

- **Nutrients**: Vitamins A, K, C, calcium, antioxidants
- **Benefits**: Detoxifying properties and help boost wellness with numerous vitamins and minerals.

## Cucumbers

- **Nutrients**: Vitamins K, C, magnesium, potassium, biotin
- **Benefits**: Low calorie, hydrating, and can help freshen a dog's breath.

When incorporating these fruits and vegetables into your dog's diet, always introduce them gradually and in moderation to see how your dog reacts, and remove any seeds or pits to avoid health issues. Some dogs may have specific dietary needs or restrictions, so it's a good idea to consult with a veterinarian before making significant changes to their diet.

## HEALTHY HOMEMADE DOG TREAT RECIPES

## MURPHY'S PEANUT BUTTER PUMPKIN TREATS

**Ingredients:**

- 2 cups whole wheat flour
- 1/2 cup pumpkin puree (not pie filling)
- 1/4 cup natural peanut butter (no xylitol or sugar added)
- 2 eggs
- 1/2 teaspoon cinnamon.

**Preparation:**

- Preheat your oven to 350°F (175°C).
- In a bowl, combine all ingredients and stir until a dough forms.
- Roll out the dough on a floured surface to about 1/4 inch thick.

- Cut into shapes with a dog treat cutter or a knife.
- Place treats on a baking sheet lined with parchment paper.
- Bake for 25 to 30 minutes until hard and golden.

**Cooking Time:** 30 minutes

**Nutritional Info (per treat):**

- Calories: 40
- Protein: 1.5g
- Fat: 1g
- Fiber: 0.8g.

**Serving Sizes:**

- Small dogs: 1 treat
- Medium dogs: 2 treats
- Large dogs: 3 treats.

## TEDDY'S SWEET POTATO AND OATS BISCUITS

**Ingredients:**

- 1 cup cooked sweet potato, mashed
- 1 3/4 cups rolled oats
- 1/3 cup chicken broth (low sodium).

**Preparation:**

- Preheat your oven to 325°F (163°C).
- Blend the oats in a food processor until they reach a flour-like consistency.
- Combine mashed sweet potato, oat flour, and chicken broth to form a dough.

- Roll out the dough and cut into desired shapes.
- Place on a parchment-lined baking sheet and bake for 35 to 40 minutes.

**Cooking Time:** 40 minutes

**Nutritional Info (per treat):**

- Calories: 30
- Protein: 1g
- Fat: 0.5g
- Fiber: 1g.

**Serving Sizes:**

- Small dogs: 1 treat
- Medium dogs: 2 treats
- Large dogs: 3 treats

## CHLOE'S APPLE CARROT CHEWS

**Ingredients:**

- 1 cup shredded apple (core and seeds removed)
- 1 cup shredded carrots
- 1 egg
- 1/4 cup unsweetened applesauce
- 1 1/2 cups whole wheat flour.

**Preparation:**

- Preheat oven to 350°F (175°C).
- Combine all ingredients in a large bowl to form a dough.
- Roll out the dough and cut into shapes or strips.

- Bake on a parchment-lined baking sheet for 30 minutes or until crisp.

**Cooking Time:** 30 minutes

**Nutritional Info (per treat):**

- Calories: 20
- Protein: 0.5g
- Fat: 0.2g
- Fiber: 0.7g.

**Serving Sizes:**

- Small dogs: 1 treat
- Medium dogs: 2 treats
- Large dogs: 3 treats.

## SOPHIE'S CHICKEN AND RICE BALLS

**Ingredients:**

- 1 cup cooked chicken, finely chopped
- 1 cup cooked brown rice
- 1 tablespoon parsley, chopped
- 1 egg.

**Preparation:**

- Preheat your oven to 350°F (175°C).
- Mix all ingredients in a bowl until well combined.
- Form small balls with the mixture.
- Place on a parchment-lined baking sheet and bake for 20 to 25 minutes or until firm and slightly golden.

**Cooking Time:** 25 minutes

**Nutritional Info (per treat):**

- Calories: 45
- Protein: 3g
- Fat: 1.5g
- Fiber: 0.5g.

**Serving Sizes:**

- Small dogs: 1 treat
- Medium dogs: 2 treats
- Large dogs: 3 treats.

## JACK'S BEEFY SPINACH SQUARES

**Ingredients:**

- 1 cup ground beef, cooked and drained
- 1/2 cup chopped spinach
- 1 cup whole wheat flour
- 2 eggs.

**Preparation:**

- Preheat oven to 350°F (175°C).
- Mix all ingredients in a bowl until well mixed.
- Press the mixture into a square baking dish.
- Bake for 20 minutes, then cut into small squares.

**Cooking Time:** 20 minutes

**Nutritional Info (per treat):**

- Calories: 50
- Protein: 4g
- Fat: 3g
- Fiber: 0.6g

**Serving Sizes:**

- Small dogs: 1 square
- Medium dogs: 2 squares
- Large dogs: 3 squares

These recipes provide a variety of flavors and textures that can cater to different tastes and dietary needs of dogs. Always introduce new treats slowly into your dog's diet and monitor for any allergic reactions or digestive issues.

## SUMMER'S DELIGHT - ICE CREAM FOR DOGS

**Ingredients:**

- 2 cups non-fat vanilla yogurt
- 1/2 cup low-fat unsalted smooth peanut butter
- 2 tablespoons honey.

**Preparation:**

**Combine Ingredients**: In a mixing bowl, combine the non-fat vanilla yogurt, low-fat unsalted smooth peanut butter, and honey. Stir until all the ingredients are well blended.

**Prepare for Freezing**: Pour the mixture into an ice cube tray or silicone mold. These molds come in various shapes like bones or paws, which can make the treats more fun for your dog.

**Freeze**: Place the tray or mold in the freezer and let it set for at least 4-6 hours, or until the mixture is completely frozen.

**Serve**: Once frozen, pop out a few "ice cream" cubes from the tray or mold and let your dog enjoy this cool treat! Be sure to feed in moderation.

**Cooking Time:** No cooking required; freeze for 4-6 hours

**Nutritional Info**

**(Per serving, approximately 1 cube):**

- Calories: 70 (this will vary based on the specific brands of ingredients used)
- Protein: 4g
- Fat: 3g
- Sugar: 4g (primarily from the honey and naturally occurring sugars in yogurt).

**Serving Sizes:**

- Small dogs: 1 cube
- Medium dogs: 2 cubes
- Large dogs: 3-4 cubes.

**Notes:**

- Always ensure that the peanut butter does not contain xylitol, which is toxic to dogs.
- The non-fat vanilla yogurt should be plain and not contain any artificial sweeteners or additives.
- You can adjust the amount of honey based on your preference or omit it if your dog is sensitive to sugar.
- Always introduce new treats gradually into your dog's diet to monitor for any digestive issues or allergies.

This homemade dog ice cream is a simple, wholesome treat that your furry friend will love during the warmer months or as a special treat. Enjoy making these delightful treats for your dog!

# KITCHEN CONVERSION CHART

| DRY MEASURES | | | | |
|---|---|---|---|---|
| GALLONS | QUARTS | PINTS | CUPS | FLUID OZ |
| 1 GAL | 4 QT | 8 PT | 16 CUP | 128 FL OZ |
| 1/2 GAL | 2 QT | 4 PT | 8 CUP | 64 FL OZ |
| 1/4 GAL | 1 QT | 2 PT | 4 CUP | 32 FL OZ |
| 1/8 GAL | 1/2 QT | 1 PT | 2 CUP | 16 FL OZ |
| 1/16 GAL | 1/4 QT | 1/2 PT | 1 CUP | 8 FL OZ |

| DRY MEASURES | | | |
|---|---|---|---|
| CUPS | TABLESPOONS | TEASPOONS | GRAMS |
| 1 CUP | 16 TBSP | 48 TSP | 229 G |
| 3/4 CUP | 12 TBSP | 36 TSP | 171 G |
| 2/3 CUP | 10 2/3 TBSP | 32 TSP | 152 G |
| 1/2 CUP | 8 TBSP | 24 TSP | 114 G |
| 1/3 CUP | 5 1/3 TBSP | 16 TSP | 76 G |
| 1/4 CUP | 4 TBSP | 12 TSP | 57 G |
| 1/8 CUP | 2 TBSP | 6 TSP | 29 G |
| 1/16 CUP | 1 TBSP | 3 TSP | 14 G |

| MEET TEMERATURES | |
|---|---|
| BEEF | |
| MEDIUM | 140°-145°F = 60°-63°C |
| MEDIUM WELL | 150°-155°F = 65°-68°C |
| WELL DONE | 160°-165°F = 71°-74°C |
| GROUND | 160°F = 71°C |
| PORK | |
| MEDIUM | 140°-145°F = 60°-63°C |
| MEDIUM WELL | 150°-155°F = 65°-68°C |
| WELL DONE | 160°-165°F = 71°-74°C |
| POULTRY | |
| ALL TYPES | 165°F = 71° |
| FISH & SEAFOOD | |
| ALL TYPES | 145°F = 60° |

OVEN TEMERATURES

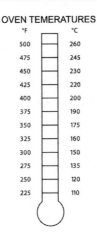

| °F | °C |
|---|---|
| 500 | 260 |
| 475 | 245 |
| 450 | 230 |
| 425 | 220 |
| 400 | 200 |
| 375 | 190 |
| 350 | 175 |
| 325 | 160 |
| 300 | 150 |
| 275 | 135 |
| 250 | 120 |
| 225 | 110 |

## TOXIC FOODS AND HOUSEHOLD ITEMS FOR DOGS

- **Chocolate**: Contains theobromine and caffeine, which are toxic to dogs and can cause heart problems, seizures, and even death.
- **Grapes and Raisins**: Can cause kidney failure in dogs. Even a small amount can make a dog ill.
- **Xylitol**: A sugar substitute found in many sugar-free products such as gum, candy, and some peanut butter. It can cause liver failure and hypoglycemia.
- **Onions and Garlic**: All forms (raw, cooked, powder, etc.) are toxic to dogs. They contain compounds that can cause gastroenteritis, anemia, and serious digestive upset.
- **Macadamia Nuts**: Contain toxins that can affect the digestive and nervous systems and muscles, leading to weakness, swelling, lethargy, vomiting, and hyperthermia.
- **Avocado**: Contains persin, which can cause vomiting and diarrhea in dogs. The pit also poses a significant choking hazard.
- **Alcohol**: Even small amounts of alcohol, including alcohol in foods, can cause ethanol poisoning in dogs, which is potentially fatal.
- **Coffee, Tea, and Other Caffeines**: Contains caffeine that can be fatal to dogs, and there is no antidote.
- **Cooked Bones**: Can splinter and cause obstruction or laceration of the digestive system.
- **Yeast Dough**: Can rise and cause gas to accumulate in your pet's digestive system. This can be painful and can cause the stomach or intestines to rupture.
- **Raw/Undercooked Meat, Eggs, and Bones**: Can contain bacteria such as Salmonella and E. coli that can be harmful to pets and humans.

- **Salt and Salty Snack Foods**: Large amounts of salt can produce excessive thirst and urination, or even sodium ion poisoning in pets.
- **Persimmons, Peaches, and Plums**: The pits from these fruits can cause inflammation of the small intestine in dogs. They also contain cyanide, which is poisonous.
- **Milk and Dairy Products**: Some adult dogs and cats may develop diarrhea if given large amounts of dairy products.
- **Fat Trimmings and Bones**: Fat trimmed from meat, both cooked and uncooked, can cause pancreatitis in dogs.
- **Citrus**: The stems, leaves, peels, fruit, and seeds of citrus plants contain varying amounts of citric acid, essential oils that can cause irritation and possibly even central nervous system depression if ingested in significant amounts.
- **Human Medications**: Common medications like ibuprofen or acetaminophen are highly toxic to pets in doses that would be considered safe for humans.

It's important to keep these foods out of your dog's reach and educate others who might be handling your pets about these dangers. If you suspect your dog has eaten any of these toxic foods, contact your veterinarian or an emergency veterinary clinic immediately.

# MAKE A DIFFERENCE WITH YOUR REVIEW

## UNLOCK THE POWER OF GENEROSITY

*"Giving is not just about making a donation. It is about making a difference."*

KATHY CALVIN

Folks who give a piece of their heart without expecting a pat on the back tend to find their lives filled with more wagging tails and wet-nosed nuzzles. You can bet your biscuits that if we can sneak a piece of that happiness pie while we are flipping through these pages together, we will certainly do so.

Here's my question for you...

**Would you toss a bone to someone you've never met, even if your pup didn't lead you to them?**

Who is this mysterious person, you wonder? Well, they're a lot like you. Maybe you, from a while back, were less seasoned in the ways of doggy dining, eager to make a difference in their furry pal's life, looking for a guiding hand but not sure which way to go to the dog park.

Our mission is to create homemade dog food that any paw parent can whip up with a flick of the tail. Everything I do, every recipe I whisk together, is for that mission. But the only way to really spread the word to every human and their hound is to reach... well... everyone.

This is where you wag in. You see, most people choose a book based on its flashy cover (as well as the woofs and wags it gets from others).

So here's my plea on behalf of a hopeful paw parent you've never met:

**Please help that dog lover by giving this book a little bark of your own.**

Your howl into the world doesn't cost a dime and takes less time than a belly rub, but it can lead a fellow dog owner to the path of nutritious, tail-waggin' goodness.

Your shout-out could help...

...one more family enjoys extra years with their playful pup.
...one more dog leap with health and happiness.
...one more human finds joy in the kitchen alongside their furry chef.
...one more four-legged friend gets a shinier coat.
...one more dream of healthy, happy pets comes true.

To get that 'pawsome' feeling and truly make a difference, all you've got to do is leave a review (yep, less than a doggy minute).

Just scan the QR code to share your thoughts:

Welcome to the pack. You're one of the good humans.

Please submit a photo of your dog wearing a bandana around their neck with your Amazon Review of my cookbook. I would love to see all of your beautiful dogs ready to eat some 'Healthy Home-made Dog Food'. I'm sure the rest of the world would love to see them also

I'm wagging with excitement to help you whip up the tastiest, healthiest meals faster than you could dream. **You're going to flip for the recipes that come up next.**

A million thanks and belly rubs. Now, let's get back to cooking up something delish.

Your biggest fan,

*Dakota O'Hare*

P.S. - Fun fact: When you toss a bone to someone else, they just might bring it back to you.

# CHAPTER 5
# TAILORING DIETS FOR THRIVING CANINES

I n the hustle and bustle of daily life, the importance of a carefully prepared meal cannot be overstated, particularly when it comes to our dogs' health. This chapter focuses on tailored dietary plans aimed at tackling common health issues, underlining how crucial proper nutrition is in ensuring our pets lead full and vibrant lives.

## 5.1 ANTI-INFLAMMATORY MEALS FOR JOINT HEALTH

### Identifying Inflammation Symptoms

A dog limping after a restful sleep or struggling to climb stairs that were once conquered with ease may signal discomfort stemming from inflammation. These subtle changes often dismissed as mere signs of aging, might indeed be the body's cry for help, indicating underlying joint inflammation or arthritis. Recognizing these symptoms early can dramatically alter the course, offering a pathway to relief through dietary adjustments.

### Anti-Inflammatory Ingredients

Nature provides a pantry full of ingredients known for their anti-inflammatory properties. Turmeric, for instance, stands out not just for its vibrant color but for curcumin, its active component, celebrated for reducing inflammation. Omega-3 fatty acids, abundant in fish like salmon and sardines, offer another powerful ally, combating inflammation at the cellular level. Incorporating green leafy vegetables such as spinachs and kales, rich in antioxidants, further supports the body's natural inflammation-fighting mechanisms.

### Recipe Ideas

A slow-cooked salmon, is always flesh flaking at the touch of a fork, infused with turmeric and ginger, served alongside a bed of steamed kale. This meal is a potent weapon against inflammation, weaving together flavors and nutrients into a tapestry of health.

Another recipe could be made by blending sardines with sweet potatoes and spinach, creating a rich, hearty stew that dogs find irresistible, not just for its taste but for the comfort it brings to their aching joints.

**Long-term Management**

Diet, which is a powerful tool in managing inflammation, works best when integrated into a healthy lifestyle. Consistent exercise, tailored to the dog's abilities and comfort level, helps maintain joint mobility and muscle strength, while regular veterinary check-ups ensure any dietary strategy aligns with the dog's evolving health needs. This multi-faceted approach, centered around an anti-inflammatory diet, can significantly improve quality of life, turning back the clock on the effects of inflammation.

**Visual Element: The Anti-Inflammatory Grocery List**

- Salmon: A source of omega-3 fatty acids, combats inflammation at the cellular level.
- Turmeric: It contains curcumin, its active component reduces inflammation.
- Ginger: Contains gingerol, a potent anti-inflammatory and antioxidant ingredient.
- Spinach: Rich in iron and antioxidants, it bolsters the immune system and offers anti-inflammatory properties.
- Kale: Rich in antioxidants, further supports the body's natural inflammation-fighting mechanisms.

## 5.2 GUT-FRIENDLY FOODS TO IMPROVE DIGESTION

Inside a dog's gastrointestinal tract lies a complex ecosystem of microorganisms which is more than just a food processing unit. This internal community of bacteria is crucial for overall health, affecting everything from how nutrients are absorbed to the immune system's efficiency. Hence, maintaining the health of this gut microbiome is not just an added benefit but a key aspect of canine care. It requires a dietary approach designed to support and safeguard this essential ecosystem.

Gut health is centered on the crucial partnership between probiotics, the friendly bacteria residing in the digestive system, and prebiotics, the indigestible fibers that nourish them. Foods rich in probiotics, such as yogurt, kefir, and fermented vegetables, play a pivotal role in nurturing this internal ecosystem, replenishing and diversifying the gut's bacterial community. These probiotic sources help strengthen the digestive system's defenses against harmful bacteria. On the other hand, foods loaded with prebiotics like chicory root, dandelion greens, and apples provide essential sustenance for these beneficial microbes, encouraging their proliferation and activity. Together, probiotics and prebiotics harmonize the gut's microbial environment, laying a solid foundation for digestive health.

The dietary landscape is riddled with potential disruptors, ingredients that, though seemingly innocuous, can incite turmoil within the gut. Grains containing gluten, for instance, often vilified in human nutrition circles, can pose similar threats to dogs, irritating the digestive tract and triggering inflammatory responses. Similarly, artificial additives, preservatives, and sweeteners, ubiquitous in commercial dog foods, may disturb the microbial equilibrium, undermining gut health and opening the door to digestive disorders.

When creating meals focused on enhancing digestive health, the range of gut-supportive foods broadens significantly. Each selection is made with the dual purpose of providing nutritional value and bolstering the digestive system. Consider a wholesome stew, simmering with lean meats, pumpkin, and an assortment of vegetables rich in prebiotics, acting as a soothing agent for the digestive tract. Or serving homemade kefir poured over fresh, diced apples and carrots for a meal that is not only refreshing but also packed with both probiotics and prebiotics, promoting a healthy gut microbiome. These dishes go beyond mere nutrition. They serve as tools for health, with every component carefully chosen for its beneficial effects on the digestive system.

The journey toward optimal gut health for our dogs is shaped by the dietary choices we make on their behalf, highlighting an often-neglected truth: true health begins not in the vet's office, but rather in the kitchen. In the act of preparing meals, we hold the key to positively influencing our dogs' health, meticulously choosing each ingredient for its beneficial impact on the gut microbiome.

## 5.3 BOOSTING IMMUNITY WITH ANTIOXIDANT-RICH RECIPES

In the world of canine nutrition, each nutrient has its specific role to play, but antioxidants are especially crucial. They act as the body's defenders against free radicals—harmful molecules generated by normal bodily processes, which can damage cells, proteins, and even DNA. This ongoing battle can lead to premature aging and disease, but antioxidants protect cellular health by neutralizing free radicals, maintaining balance, and preventing damage.

Antioxidants are not just supplements; it's about recognizing their essential role in immune health. These molecules varied in their makeup but united in their mission, giving up electrons to free radicals, stopping them in their tracks, and preventing widespread cellular damage. This process doesn't deplete the antioxidants; instead, they remain active in the body, continually ready to defend against new assaults. The impact on a dog's immune system is significant, with antioxidants strengthening defenses against germs, easing inflammation, and helping to mend injured tissues. Therefore, incorporating foods rich in antioxidants into your dog's diet is not just about providing nutrition; it's about fortifying their body against the diverse challenges it encounters every day.

The variety of antioxidants parallels the diversity of their food sources, each contributing uniquely to a dog's health. Berries, bursting with color and sweetness, are packed with antioxidants like vitamin C and flavonoids that help fight inflammation and boost the immune system. Carrots and sweet potatoes, are rich in beta-carotene that are converted in the body to vitamin A, crucial for protecting mucous membranes and warding off infections. Leafy greens such as kale and spinach are loaded with nutrients including lutein and zeaxanthin which are essential for maintaining sharp vision, ensuring a dog's eyes are as keen as their sense of hearing.

Incorporating a range of antioxidant-rich foods into your dog's diet is crucial for their overall health. This dietary variety serves two purposes: it wards off the potential for mealtime boredom and guarantees a comprehensive array of antioxidants, each essential for different aspects of your dog's well-being. A dish that combines crispness of kale with the natural sweetness of blueberries and the hearty depth of sweet potatoes isn't just a treat for their taste buds but a powerful mix of nutrients that supports the immune system at every level.

A purée of pumpkin and pear breakfast, drizzled with a touch of flaxseed oil, offering a blend of vitamins A, C, and E, alongside omega-3 fatty acids. Dinner could be a lightly cooked salmon, rich in astaxanthin, served alongside a quinoa and berry salad, dressed in a light vinaigrette. Such meals, though simple, are potent in their nutritional value, each ingredient selected not only for its inherent antioxidants but for its ability to synergize with others, amplifying the protective effects across the body.

In this approach to canine nutrition, where antioxidants play a starring role, the focus shifts from feeding to nourishing, from the mere act of satiation to the profound act of care. It acknowledges that every meal is an opportunity to reinforce the body's defenses, to lay down arms against the inevitable wear of time and disease. Through the strategic incorporation of antioxidant-rich foods into daily meals, we not only cater to the gustatory delights of our canine companions but arm them against the unseen foes that threaten them from within.

## 5.4 CANINE DETOX: CLEAN MEALS TO RESET YOUR DOG'S HEALTH

Within dog nutrition, the idea of a detox diet frequently stands out as a path to rejuvenation, cutting through the buildup of toxins that might diminish a dog's energy and health. This approach, is deeply rooted in the essential need to bolster the organs charged with detoxification, ensuring they function at their best. For dogs living in cities, consuming processed foods, or recuperating from sickness, a well-designed detox diet can serve as a powerful tool, revitalizing their system and clearing out the remnants of contemporary life.

Most signs could suggest that your dog might benefit from this dietary adjustment, from subtle hints like decreased energy and a dull coat to more noticeable issues such as digestive problems and ongoing skin irritations. These diverse symptoms all stem from a common cause: the body's need for a break from dietary overindulgences and environmental pollutants. Within this framework, the detox diet is introduced not as a cure-all but as a thoughtful pause, designed to help the body repair and revitalize.

The foundation of a detox diet is built on the key principles of simplicity and purity. When crafting such a diet, it's important to focus on whole, minimally processed foods that are nutrient-dense yet easy on the digestive system. Ingredients selected for their natural detoxifying properties, such as leafy greens, lean proteins, and a handpicked assortment of fruits and vegetables, support the body's detox pathways without overwhelming it. This approach is all about finding a balance, allowing for the removal of toxins while ensuring the body is nourished with essential nutrients, thereby maintaining a crucial balance necessary for optimal health and recovery.

Central to the detox diet's efficacy is its support for the liver and kidneys, the stalwart organs that bear the brunt of detoxification. Foods that elevate this diet from mere sustenance to a therapeutic tool include milk thistle, known for its hepatoprotective qualities, and dandelion greens, a natural diuretic that aids kidney function. The inclusion of cruciferous vegetables like broccoli and Brussels sprouts introduces compounds that enhance liver's capacity to neutralize toxins, while the modest cranberry, with its urinary tract benefits, supports kidney health. This dietary blending tradition with science, fortifies the body's natural defenses, ensuring the seamless elimination of toxins while safeguarding against oxidative stress.

The transition from a detox diet back to a broader range of foods demands attentiveness and care. Initially, the reintroduction of previously eliminated foods occurs one at a time, allowing for the observation of any adverse reactions, a method that respects the individual dog's tolerance and response. This careful, deliberate expansion of the diet ensures that the benefits accrued during the detox phase are not undone but rather built upon, setting the stage for a sustainable dietary pattern that continues to support detoxification and overall health.

Central to this strategy is the recognition that a detox diet is merely one component of a comprehensive approach to canine wellness. It doesn't serve as the ultimate solution but rather as a vital stepping-stone towards revitalizing a dog's health. By carefully selecting pure and wholesome foods, this diet functions as a powerful reset button, refreshing the body's systems and reigniting the natural vitality inherent to all dogs.

## 5.5 LOW-ALLERGEN MEALS FOR SENSITIVE DOGS

In the world of dog care, food allergies, and sensitivities present a significant challenge, often overshadowing the joy of feeding time. For dogs dealing with these issues, every meal could lead to discomfort, turning what should be a pleasurable experience into a source of stress. Identifying these allergies demands careful attention, requiring owners to notice and interpret the subtle signs of discomfort their dogs may show. Unable to communicate their pain directly, dogs express their distress through physical symptoms such as constant scratching, skin irritation, or a noticeable lack of energy after eating. These symptoms, which might be easily overlooked as minor or unrelated issues, are actually critical indicators of a deeper problem needing attention.

The path to isolating allergens through diet introduces pet owners to the elimination diet, a methodical approach that strips down meals to their most basic components. Starting with a limited ingredient diet, typically consisting of a single protein source and one carbohydrate, unfamiliar to the dog, will set the stage for investigation. Over weeks, this controlled feeding reveals its value, as the absence of common allergens gradually unveils the culprit through the absence of symptoms. The reintroduction of ingredients, one at a time, with a vigilant eye on the dog's reactions, further narrows down the list of potential allergens, transforming the diet from a broad spectrum to a targeted strike against the sources of discomfort.

The range of low-allergen ingredients forms a diverse palette, ensuring that meals are not just safe but also appealing and flavorful. Uncommon proteins like venison, rabbit, and kangaroo offer nutritious alternatives that avoid the common allergens found in beef and chicken. For grains, options like tapioca and sweet potatoes provide energy without introducing gluten or the allergenic components typically found in wheat, corn, or soy. Choosing these ingredients based on their low potential for allergies paints a dietary scene where nourishment and safety are seamlessly intertwined.

A diet devoid of allergens is a careful process of balance and attentive observation. This approach to dietary management goes beyond simply avoiding certain foods, and incorporating supplements and alternative nutrient sources to achieve comprehensive nutrition. To counteract the restricted variety in protein, omega-3 fatty acids from sources like fish oil or flaxseeds are recommended to enhance skin health. Additionally, the introduction of probiotics and fiber from ingredients such as pumpkin or beet pulp strengthens digestive wellness, safeguarding the gut against sensitivity issues. This flexible adjustment of the diet, tailored to meet the dog's evolving needs and observations, reflects the nuanced strategy required to manage allergies effectively.

## 5.6 RECIPES TO SUPPORT ORAL HEALTH AND FRESHEN BREATH

The dialogue between a dog's diet and the vitality of their oral health unfolds in a nuanced interplay of ingredients, textures, and routines. This relationship, starts at the intersection of nutrition and dental care, suggests that what we choose to feed our pets can either contribute to or detract from the robustness of their gums, the strength of their teeth, and the freshness of their breath. It suggests that meals and treats can act as allies in the pursuit of oral hygiene, working together with regular dental care practices to ensure a mouth free of disease and discomfort.

Creation of chewable meals and treats emerges as an act of preventive care, transforming the act of eating into an opportunity for mechanical cleaning. The physical action required to break down certain foods can effectively massage the gums and scour the teeth, dislodging plaque and food particles that, if left unattended, could foster bacteria and lead to periodontal disease. Raw vegetables like carrots and celery, with their fibrous texture, serve this purpose well, offering a natural abrasive that cleans without harming the enamel. Similarly, homemade treats crafted from dehydrated meats require vigorous chewing, providing a satisfying and beneficial workout for the teeth and gums.

The incorporation of ingredients known for their breath-freshening properties further elevates the dental benefits of a dog's diet. Parsley, with its chlorophyll content, is renowned for neutralizing bad odors, while coconut oil, lauded for its antimicrobial properties, can help reduce bacteria levels in the mouth, a common culprit behind halitosis. Peppermint and dill, used sparingly, can impart a pleasant aroma, combatting the often pungent aftermath of a meal. These ingredients, when added to daily meals or formulated into special treats, interweave the benefits of fresh breath with the overall nutritional profile of the diet, ensuring that oral hygiene does not stand apart but is seamlessly integrated into the fabric of daily feeding practices.

However, it's important to understand that these dietary strategies should complement a comprehensive oral healthcare routine. Consistent brushing with dog-specific toothpaste is the foundation of good dental hygiene, effectively preventing plaque from turning into tartar.

Professional cleanings by a veterinarian at least once a year are essential for deep dental cleansing, targeting areas that daily brushing can't reach and ensuring the complete removal of plaque and tartar. This blend of dietary measures and dental care practices highlights the fact that achieving a healthy mouth involves a consistent, integrated routine.

In crafting recipes, one might consider a simple blend of minced parsley and coconut oil, frozen into small cubes that offer a refreshing treat post-meal, aiding in digestion while freshening breath. Another option could involve forming patties from ground turkey mixed with finely chopped mint and dill, baked until crisp. These patties, served as part of a meal or as an occasional treat, not only satisfy the palate but engage the teeth and gums in a beneficial cleaning exercise.

From the insights of this chapter, there is a clear message: our choices in ingredients and routines significantly affect our dogs' health and happiness. We learn that our role is much more than just a caretaker; we are advocates and allies for our pets, equipped with the knowledge and tools to help them not just survive but thrive. This chapter has shown us that meals can be more than just nourishing—they can heal, clean, and rejuvenate. As we move forward, it's crucial to remember the powerful impact we have on our dogs' lives with every meal we prepare and every routine we follow, always keeping in mind the trust they place in us.

# CHAPTER 6
# NURTURING VITALITY WITH NATURE'S BOUNTY

W e are living in a world where synthetic solutions often overshadow nature's offerings. In light to this, spotlight rarely falls on the humble yet powerful superfoods. These nutritional powerhouses, though unassuming in appearance, pack a punch, offering a variety of health benefits that can significantly enhance our dogs' well-being. For example, blueberries although small and unpretentious are brimming with antioxidants, and pumpkin with its fibrous flesh supports digestive health. These are not just ingredients; they are nature's tools for vitality, each bearing gifts that extend far beyond their size or origins.

## 6.1 SUPERFOODS FOR DOGS: WHAT THEY ARE AND HOW TO USE THEM

### Definition and Benefits

Superfoods have become a cornerstone in discussions about nutrition, denoting foods brimming with nutrients and antioxidants. These foods deliver an array of benefits including bolstered immune function, better digestive health, increased energy, and a shield against diseases. Rich in essential vitamins, minerals, and antioxidants, superfoods serve as a powerful complement to a dog's diet, offering both preventative health advantages and a daily enhancement of well-being.

### List of Canine Superfoods

- **Blueberries**: Loaded with antioxidants, they combat free radicals, supporting cellular health and reducing the risk of chronic diseases.
- **Pumpkin**: High in fiber and low in calories, it aids in digestive health and weight management.
- **Carrots**: Crunchy and full of beta-carotene, they support eye health and provide a dental health benefit through mechanical chewing action.
- **Spinach**: Rich in iron and antioxidants, it bolsters the immune system and offers anti-inflammatory properties.

- **Sardines**: A source of omega-3 fatty acids, they promote skin and coat health while supporting cognitive function.

## Incorporating Superfoods into Meals

Adding superfoods to your dog's diet can be as simple as sprinkling blueberries over their morning meal or mixing mashed pumpkin into their dinner. Consider replacing commercial treats with sliced carrots for a crunchy, nutritious snack. For those looking to enhance their dog's omega-3 intake, a sardine once or twice a week can make a significant difference. The key is having a variety and moderation, ensuring your dog reaps the benefits without the risk of nutrient imbalances.

## Monitoring Reactions

Introducing new foods into your dog's diet should always be a gradual process, allowing time to observe any adverse reactions. Start with small amounts and pay attention to signs of digestive upset or allergic reactions, such as itching or changes in bowel movements. Remember, what works for one dog may not work for another; customization based on individual tolerance and preferences is crucial.

## 6.2 THE BENEFITS OF FERMENTED FOODS IN A DOG'S DIET

Fermented foods stand out as understated, yet powerful contributors, often overshadowed by more commonly recognized dietary elements. Fermentation, a natural process driven by bacteria and yeasts, transforms food in a way that unlocks a range of nutrients that were previously locked away in raw ingredients. This time-honored method of preservation, celebrated in various cultures, brings significant health advantages to dogs, aligning seamlessly with their body's needs and enhancing overall wellness.

Fermented foods for dogs, much like those for humans, span a diverse range, each with its unique flavor profile and health benefits. Kefir and fermented vegetables stand out as beacons in this category, their consumption linked to enhanced digestive health and a fortified immune system. Kefir, a fermented milk product, teems with probiotics, the beneficial bacteria that colonize the gut, creating a bulwark against pathogens while aiding in nutrient absorption. Fermented vegetables, on the other hand, offers a crunch that dogs relish, their fibers pre-digested by the fermentation process, making them an excellent source of vitamins and minerals.

Begin with small servings, a teaspoon of kefir, or a few shreds of fermented vegetables, to gauge tolerance. This incremental strategy allows the dog's digestive system to acclimate to the influx of probiotics, minimizing the risk of gastrointestinal upset. Observing your dog's reaction to these initial servings provides invaluable feedback, guiding further adjustments in quantity and frequency. The goal is a seamless integration of fermented foods into the diet, one that enhances rather than disrupts, nurturing the dog's health from within.

By incorporating probiotics through fermented foods, we cultivate a diverse and sturdy bacterial environment in the digestive system. This diversity is crucial, as each type of bacteria offers unique benefits, including immune system enhancement, essential vitamin production, and the breakdown of difficult plant fibers. Furthermore, the mild acidity of these foods rich in probiotics acts as a deterrent to harmful bacteria growth, fostering a balanced gut and promoting overall health.

In this context, fermented foods go beyond being simple dietary components. Their integration into a dog's diet reflects a comprehensive philosophy that recognizes the deep connection between gut health and the immune system, alongside mental and physical well-being. Nurturing the gut ensures our dogs do more than just survive—they thrive in a delicate equilibrium between wellness and disease.

## 6.3 INTEGRATING HERBAL SUPPLEMENTS SAFELY

The world of herbal supplements offers a range of benefits to canine health, from increasing energy levels to alleviating everyday discomforts. The natural potency of these remedies can lead to positive health outcomes as well as potential risks if not used correctly. It's essential to have a thorough understanding of each supplement's effects, proper usage, and correct dosages to ensure they contribute positively to your dog's health plan, avoiding any negative side effects from overuse.

Herbal supplements for dogs, much like those utilized in human health, originate from the earth's flora. Each plant, leaf, and root, carries within its cells a history of medicinal use that spans cultures and centuries. From the soothing embrace of chamomile, known for its calming properties, to the gentle detoxification offered by milk thistle, these supplements speak a language of healing and harmony. Turmeric, with its vibrant hue, stands as a testament to nature's alchemy, offering anti-inflammatory properties that rival synthetic alternatives. Similarly, the adaptogenic qualities of ashwagandha support endocrine health, offering a buffer against the stresses that fray the edges of well-being.

The introduction of these botanicals into a dog's diet must first and foremost align with an understanding of each herb's specific benefits and potential interactions. For instance, chamomile, while generally safe, might interact with sedative medications, necessitating a dialogue between natural remedies and pharmaceutical interventions. Similarly, the administration of turmeric, though beneficial for its anti-inflammatory effects, requires moderation to avoid gastrointestinal upset, illustrating the balance necessary between therapeutic benefit and the dog's overall dietary harmony.

Administering these supplements has its roots in the principle of gradual integration. Starting with minimal doses allows for the observation of the dog's response, both in terms of efficacy and potential adverse reactions. This cautious approach not only respects the potent nature of herbal remedies but also acknowledges the unique physiological landscape of each canine. A small sprinkle of ground turmeric over food or a few drops of chamomile extract in water represents a starting point, from which adjustments can be made based on observed outcomes.

The guidance of a veterinarian provides a compass by which the suitability of specific supplements can be assessed. This professional insight is invaluable, offering a perspective that considers the dog's overall health, existing conditions, and current medications to ensure the safe and effective use of herbal remedies. Such consultations might reveal nuances in a dog's health that necessitate adjustments in supplement choice or dosage, tailoring the approach to herbal supplementation to fit the individual needs of the canine.

The journey does not end at the point of selection or even administration of supplements. It extends into a continuous cycle of observation, adjustment, and dialogue, a triad that ensures the safe and beneficial use of nature's pharmacy in enhancing canine health. Through this approach, the green world of herbal supplements unfolds not as a panacea but as a tool to support and enhance the well-being of our canine companions.

## 6.4 THE ROLE OF PROBIOTICS AND PREBIOTICS

Probiotics and prebiotics play roles that are as critical as they are complementary, forming a symbiotic alliance that underpins not just digestive wellness but also the broader spectrum of canine health. Probiotics, live beneficial bacteria, take up residence in the gut, where their presence curbs the growth of harmful bacteria, aiding in nutrient absorption and contributing to a robust immune system. Prebiotics, on the other hand, are dietary fibers that the body cannot digest. They serve as nourishment for these probiotic bacteria, fostering a gut environment where these beneficial microbes can flourish.

The sources from which dogs can obtain these vital components are as varied as they are natural. For probiotics, fermented products stand out—kefir, a fermented milk drink, and certain types of yogurt, unsweetened and without artificial additives, are prime examples. These provide a direct supply of live cultures that can bolster the population of good bacteria in the gut. For prebiotics, the focus shifts to fibrous foods that resist digestion, reaching the colon intact to feed probiotic bacteria. Chicory root, beet pulp, and inulin, a component found in asparagus, bananas, and garlic, are potent prebiotic sources, acting as the fuel that probiotics need to thrive.

The benefits of this dynamic duo extend far beyond the confines of the gut. A well-populated microbiome, supported by a steady supply of prebiotics, plays a pivotal role in digestive health, ensuring smooth processing of food and efficient waste elimination. Beyond digestion, the presence of a healthy bacterial population influences the immune system. The gut, home to a significant portion of the body's immune cells, becomes a site of intense activity where probiotics interact with immune cells, training them and modulating responses to pathogens. This interaction not only heightens the body's ability to fend off infections but can also temper allergic reactions, making a well-maintained gut a corner-stone of overall health.

Starting with prebiotics, and introducing fibrous foods should be a gradual process. An abrupt increase can lead to a digestive upset, as the gut adjusts to the additional fiber. A slice of banana here, and a sprinkling of beet pulp there, allows the dog's system to adapt without discomfort. For probiotics, the key lies in ensuring the survival of these beneficial bacteria until they reach the gut. Opt for cold dishes where live cultures are less likely to be destroyed by heat, mixing probiotics into cold, wet food or offering them as part of a cooling snack.

Incorporating probiotics and prebiotics into a dog's diet goes beyond simply adding new ingredients; it's about creating an environment where these vital components can thrive and perform their essential functions. This approach is a dedication to enhancing the often-overlooked, yet crucial, ecosystem within a dog's gut. This dedication allows us to offer more than mere nutrients; we lay down a foundation for a life filled with vitality and well-being, one meal at a time.

## 6.5 CUSTOMIZING DIETS FOR ATHLETIC AND WORKING DOGS

In the dynamic world of athletic and working dogs, the demands placed upon their bodies transcend the ordinary, pushing the boundaries of endurance, strength, and agility. These dogs, whether they grace the agility course with their acrobatic feats or patrol with unwavering diligence, engage in activities that consume vast reserves of energy, necessitating a diet meticulously engineered to fuel their endeavors and facilitate recovery. This canine nutrition, where performance intersects with vitality, requires an approach that is both precise and adaptable, attuning to the nuanced demands of the athletic canine body.

The dialogue surrounding the increased nutritional needs of these active dogs often centers on the critical balance of energy intake and expenditure. The elevated caloric demands, a direct consequence of their vigorous activities, call for a diet that not only satisfies but sustains a steady stream of energy derived from quality sources. Carbohydrates, while sometimes viewed with skepticism in the context of standard canine diets, emerge here as invaluable allies, offering quick-release energy that fuels short bursts of intense activity. Yet, the reliance on carbohydrates is a calibrated affair, emphasizing complex forms like sweet potatoes and brown rice that release energy gradually, avoiding the peaks and troughs associated with simpler sugars.

Proteins, the bedrock of muscle repair and growth, assume a role of heightened importance in the diet of the athletic dog. The rigorous demands of their activities inflict microscopic injuries upon muscle fibers, necessitating a rich supply of amino acids for repair and strengthening. Here, the quality of the protein source becomes paramount, with lean meats, eggs, and fish providing the full spectrum of essential amino acids required for optimal muscle recovery. This focus on high-quality protein not only supports the physical demands placed upon these dogs but also aids in maintaining lean muscle mass, a critical factor in ensuring agility and preventing injury.

The integration of supplements into the diet of athletic and working dogs offers a layer of support that complements the foundational nutrients provided by their meals. Omega-3 fatty acids, derived from fish oil or flaxseed, lend their anti-inflammatory properties to support joint health, a concern of paramount importance for dogs engaged in high-impact activities. Glucosamine and chondroitin, often heralded for their role in maintaining cartilage and joint fluid, become not just beneficial but essential for dogs whose activities place significant stress upon their joints. These supplements, when introduced thoughtfully and in appropriate dosages, act not as mere additions but as integral components of a holistic dietary strategy aimed at optimizing performance and ensuring longevity in their active roles.

Yet, the meticulous crafting of these diets, enriched with targeted nutrients and supplements, finds its true measure in the practice of regular monitoring and adjustments. The needs of athletic and working dogs are not static but evolve with the intensity of their training schedules, the changing of seasons, and the natural aging process. Continuous observation becomes a tool of unparalleled value, enabling the discerning eye to catch the subtle signs of nutritional imbalance or deficiency. A coat that loses its luster, a performance that falters, or a recovery that lengthens, each serves as a quiet signal, prompting a reassessment of the dietary regimen. This dynamic process of monitoring, coupled with the readiness to adjust the diet in response to these cues, ensures that the nutritional strategy remains aligned with the dog's current needs, supporting their health and performance across the spectrum of their activities.

When we ensure the vitality of athletic and working dogs through proper nutrition, their diet shifts from a basic necessity to a pivotal element in their life story. This shift underscores the concept that peak performance stems not just from rigorous training but from a holistic approach to care, with nutrition playing a foundational role. By adopting a tailored and flexible nutrition plan, we recognize and cater to each dog's unique needs as we honor their relentless spirit.

## 6.6 NUTRIENT-RICH TREATS AND SNACKS

In this act of crafting treats, we use simple ingredients to create healthful treasures, a clear sign of our deep love for our pets. Here, in the warmth of our kitchens, we start enhancing our dogs' diets with delicious, nutrient-packed snacks.

The world of healthy treats reveals a treasure trove of natural ingredients, each bringing its unique flavors and nutritional benefits to our dogs' diets. Take the apple, for example; its crisp, sweet flesh wrapped in fiber-rich skin makes for a deliciously satisfying treat that also supports digestive health. Then there's the sweet potato, transformed through dehydration into chewy slices that not only delight the taste buds but also supply essential vitamins A and C, nurturing the skin, coat, and vision. Also, lean chicken which when baked and shredded, offers a lean, protein-rich snack that aids in muscle health and recovery. These treats, crafted from straightforward, nutritious ingredients, merge the joys of taste with the essentials of health, ensuring every bite is a step towards enhanced vitality for our dogs.

Choosing homemade treats over commercial options goes beyond just ensuring the quality of ingredients. It's a step towards freedom from the hidden additives, preservatives, and often unclear ingredients that fill the labels of store-bought snacks. By preparing snacks at home, you gain complete transparency over what goes into your dog's treats, allowing you to customize them according to your dog's dietary needs, allergies, or health concerns. This personal touch not only enriches the nutritional value of the treats, but also strengthens the bond between you and your pet through the very act of preparation and feeding.

Balancing the intake of treats with regular meals demands a mindful approach, one that ensures these culinary delights complement rather than compete with the diet's nutritional goals. A guideline emerges from this need for balance, suggesting treats should not exceed ten percent of the dog's daily caloric intake. Adherence to this guideline maintains the equilibrium of diet, ensuring treats remain a source of pleasure and health rather than disruption.

Frozen broth cubes, enriched with herbs and bits of meat, transform a summer day's training session into a refreshing reward. A puzzle feeder, loaded with homemade treats, turns snack time into an engaging activity, stimulating the mind as well as the palate. These innovations in snacking not only enrich the dog's diet but enhance their daily experiences, turning moments of feeding into opportunities for growth, learning, and bonding.

As we wrap up our exploration of nutrient-rich treats and snacks, it becomes clear that these homemade delights are not just treats but pivotal elements of our dogs' nutrition. Each recipe, crafted with both love and science, stands as a testament to the extraordinary care we put into our pets' health. These treats are more than simple indulgences; they're crucial components of a well-rounded diet, reflecting our deep commitment to our pets' health and happiness.

# CHAPTER 7
# NURTURING ADAPTABILITY IN CANINE DIETS

E xploring the nutritional adaptability for our dogs can often feel like journeying through an uncharted wilderness. Each step brings an opportunity to refine the balance of flavors, textures, and nutrients that make up their meals. Here we learn to navigate the complexities of picky eating—transforming it from a simple matter of taste to an understanding of our dogs' distinct preferences.

## 7.1 OVERCOMING PICKY EATING: TIPS AND TRICKS

### Introduction of Variety

The monotony of the same meals, day in and day out, dulls the excitement of dining—a truth not exclusive to humans. For dogs faced with an unchanging menu, the zest for mealtime wanes, a signal not of ingratitude but a plea for diversity. Imagine the transition from a diet that has never strayed beyond the boundaries of chicken and rice to the introduction of lamb, beef, or even exotic proteins like kangaroo. This shift revitalizes and invites renewed interest with each meal.

In practical terms, rotating the protein source every few weeks or incorporating a variety of vegetables can transform the dining experience.

### Mealtime Routines

Consistency, the backbone of any successful endeavor, finds its place at the dining table as well. Setting a regular schedule for meals offers a framework within which anticipation and appetite can grow. It's the difference between a hastily grabbed sandwich on the run and a meal savored at a table set with care—the former forgotten, the latter anticipated and remembered. This routine, once established, becomes a ritual, a time of bonding and enjoyment that elevates the act of feeding beyond mere sustenance.

**Enhancing Food Appeal**

The allure of a meal can often be captured in its aroma and presentation—a truth that holds for dogs as much as for their human counterparts. A drizzle of salmon oil, a sprinkle of finely chopped herbs, or the addition of warm, low-sodium broth can elevate a meal from ordinary to extraordinary. This strategy, leveraging natural flavor enhancers, taps into the primal senses, coaxing the pickiest eaters to reconsider their stance.

For those meals that seem to lack appeal, simple warming can release the aromas trapped within, spreading a scent that beckons even the most indifferent.

**Patience and Persistence**

Navigating the preferences of a picky eater demands patience. It's the resolve to not replace a balanced meal with treats or table scraps simply for the sake of seeing an empty bowl. This journey, celebrates small victories and learns from the setbacks.

## 7.2 ADJUSTING PORTIONS FOR WEIGHT GAIN OR LOSS

Adjusting a dog's diet for weight loss or gain requires careful consideration and flexibility, striking a balance between careful measurement and attentive observation. Tailoring a diet to meet specific goals, whether it's to reduce or increase weight, is a commitment to promoting the best possible health for your dog, acknowledging that every dog has unique energy needs that reflect their individual personality.

**Calculating Caloric Needs**

The first crucial step in tailor-making your dog's diet involves calculating their daily caloric needs. This isn't just about crunching numbers; it's about considering your dog's current condition and goal weight. The calculation is nuanced, taking into account the dog's metabolic rate, which can vary with size, breed, and age, making the caloric needs as unique as your dog. While tools and formulas created by veterinary nutritionists provide a good starting point, they are guides to begin with. The real key to success lies in applying these figures in real life and adjusting based on your dog's response.

## Monitoring Weight Changes

The pursuit of a weight goal, whether shedding excess pounds or building muscle mass, unfolds over time, not in the immediacy of days but through the steady progression of weeks and months. Regular weigh-ins, conducted with a frequency that respects the gradual nature of weight change, provides snapshots of progress, capturing the incremental victories and setbacks that mark the path toward the goal. This ritual of measurement, far from a mere administrative task, reflects a deep engagement with the dog's health journey and offering insights that inform subsequent dietary adjustments. It's a practice that, while grounded in the objective data of scales, is elevated by the subjective assessment of the dog's vitality, mobility, and overall well-being.

## Adjusting Portion Sizes

Once we've determined the caloric needs and have a system to keep track of changes, adjusting meal sizes becomes a key part of managing your dog's diet. This step requires a thoughtful approach, as it's not just about the calories but also how your dog reacts to the amount they're fed. Based on the outcomes of regular weigh-ins and observing your dog's energy levels, you may need to modify meal sizes accordingly. This process isn't about sticking strictly to predefined portions but about being adaptable and adjusting food amounts to meet your dog's ongoing needs. This ensures every meal moves your dog closer to achieving optimal health.

Adjusting the frequency of meals is equally critical. For dogs aiming to lose weight, distributing their daily caloric intake across multiple smaller meals can be advantageous, as it helps in maintaining consistent energy levels and keeps hunger at bay. On the other hand, for dogs that need to gain weight, it might be more effective to serve fewer, but more nutrient-packed meals. This approach can support muscle growth and weight gain without overburdening their digestive system.

## Incorporating Exercise

While adjusting your dog's diet is key to managing their weight, incorporating the right amount of physical activity is equally important. For dogs that need to lose weight, pairing dietary changes with increased exercise can significantly boost the calorie deficit, helping them reach their weight goals faster. However, it's vital to consider the dog's present fitness level, gradually increasing the intensity and duration of their exercise to prevent overexertion. This careful approach ensures a balanced path to weight loss, blending nutrition and physical activity for holistic health improvement.

For dogs wanting to gain weight, particularly in muscle, the focus shifts to strength-building exercises that promote muscle growth without burning too many calories. This delicate balance between nutrition and physical activity requires a comprehensive approach, considering the dog as a whole. Achieving true health comes from combining a well-nourished body with an active lifestyle, ensuring both diet and exercise work in harmony for the dog's well-being.

Navigating the balance of portion control, observing your dog's health progress, and matching their diet with appropriate exercises are key to personalized nutrition. This journey, deeply rooted in understanding your dog's specific caloric and physical activity needs, goes beyond mere numbers to touch the heart of individualized care. With every meal adjustment and exercise tweak, we demonstrate our commitment to our dogs' health—aiming not just for adequate nutrition but for their overall well-being. This path to health is dynamic, requiring constant attention and adaptability to meet our dogs' changing needs, a testament to the deep bond and trust between us and our beloved pets.

## 7.3 RECOGNIZING AND RESPONDING TO FOOD ALLERGIES

In the journey of feeding and taking care of our dogs, the issue of food allergies often emerges, leading to discomfort and unease. These allergic reactions are the body's way of indicating that certain ingredients don't agree with them, showing up through various symptoms. It's crucial to recognize these early signs to adjust their diet to meet their health requirements, making sure every meal is both nourishing and safe.

The early signs of a food allergy in dogs are not always immediately apparent, as they can resemble symptoms of less serious conditions. This subtlety can make it difficult to recognize the true issue at hand. Common manifestations includes a persistent itch leading to a non-stop scratching, the development of hot spots on the skin, or ongoing ear infections without a clear cause. Additionally, some dogs may experience gastrointestinal distress, including frequent vomiting or diarrhea, signaling a possible adverse reaction to specific foods. These diverse symptoms represent the body's way of signaling distress, calling for careful attention and appropriate action.

Starting an elimination diet is a systematic way to pinpoint what's causing your dog's food allergies. This method simplifies their diet to just one protein and one carbohydrate, usually something they haven't eaten before, to lower the chances of an allergic reaction. By removing complex ingredients found in a regular dog food, this diet acts as a clean slate, making it easier to identify the allergen.

Over several weeks, sticking to this basic diet can help you notice if your dog's symptoms improve, indicating the allergen isn't part of this simple meal plan.

Once symptoms have subsided, carefully reintroduce ingredients one at a time to test for tolerance. Monitor your dog for a week after adding each new food to watch for any allergic reactions. This careful, though gradual, approach helps in pinpointing the exact allergens to be eliminated from your dog's diet in the future.

Identifying and introducing safe, nutritious alternatives to commonly problematic allergens is an essential next step. For dogs that react to grains, alternatives like quinoa or sweet potatoes can provide similar nutritional benefits without triggering allergies. When it comes to proteins, consider hypoallergenic options such as rabbit, duck, or hydrolyzed proteins, which are broken down into smaller components that are unlikely to cause an immune reaction, instead of traditional proteins like chicken or beef. This approach not only helps in mitigating allergic symptoms but also plays a vital role in ensuring a balanced and diverse diet, which is key to maintaining overall health.

Successfully managing your dog's diet after identifying allergens demands careful, ongoing vigilance. It's not enough to simply avoid the ingredients that cause reactions; it's equally important to continuously evaluate the diet's overall nutritional value. This ensures that avoiding certain foods doesn't lead to nutritional deficiencies. Regularly consulting with a veterinary nutritionist can be incredibly beneficial, as they provide valuable advice on alternative nutrient sources and make necessary adjustments to your dog's diet plan to meet their changing nutritional needs. Adopting this vigilant approach, along with being mindful about introducing new treats or supplements, helps prevent accidental allergen exposure. This careful balance, maintained after the elimination diet, is key to safeguarding your dog's health and well-being.

In adopting a proactive approach to managing food allergies in dogs, we move away from merely reacting to symptoms and towards a focus on prevention and careful dietary adjustment. This strategy aims not just to relieve the discomfort of allergic reactions but to restore dietary balance and well-being. By meticulously monitoring symptoms, implementing an elimination diet with precision, and choosing alternative ingredients wisely, we tackle the complexities of food allergies head-on. Despite the challenges, our dedication to our dogs' health guides us through, ensuring their diets are as nourishing as they are enjoyable.

## 7.4 DEALING WITH DIGESTIVE UPSETS: DIARRHEA AND CONSTIPATION

Digestive issues in dogs, primarily seen as diarrhea and constipation, are often indicators of deeper health or dietary concerns. While these conditions are relatively common, they shouldn't be taken lightly due to their potential to cause significant discomfort or lead to more serious health problems. Successfully managing these issues requires a keen ability to recognize early signs and causes, followed by making thoughtful dietary changes. It's also essential to know when these symptoms warrant a visit to the vet. Additionally, taking steps to prevent such digestive upsets can reduce their occurrence and severity, making for a smoother experience in managing your dog's digestive health.

### Identifying Causes

The digestive discomfort in dogs can often be traced back to several issues, ranging from dietary indiscretion—those instances where dogs ingest food or objects they shouldn't—to more insidious causes such as infections, parasites, or chronic conditions like inflammatory bowel disease. The challenge lies not in listing these potential causes but in discerning which is at play in a given situation. Diarrhea, characterized by loose or watery stools, may indicate the ingestion of spoiled food, an allergic reaction, or, in more grave scenarios, diseases such as parvovirus. Constipation, on the other hand, with its infrequent or difficult bowel movements, might stem from dehydration, inadequate fiber intake, or obstructions in the digestive tract.

The task of identifying these causes begins with a careful observation of symptoms, coupled with a thorough review of recent changes in diet, behavior, or environment. A dog that has had access to garbage, for instance, or has recently been introduced to a new food, might provide clues pointing towards dietary indiscretion as the root cause of their distress.

**Dietary Solutions**

Once the likely cause of the digestive upset has been pinpointed, the path to alleviation often lies through dietary adjustments. For diarrhea, simplifying the diet to a bland, easily digestible meal—boiled chicken and rice, for example—can offer the gastrointestinal tract the respite it needs to recover. Small, frequent meals further assist in this gentle reintroduction to normal feeding. Hydration, a critical concern especially in cases of diarrhea, requires vigilant monitoring, with fresh water always available, and in some situations, the addition of an electrolyte solution to prevent dehydration.

Constipation may benefit from an increase in dietary fiber, an element found in pumpkin or wheat bran, which can help to soften stools and promote regular bowel movements. Ensuring adequate water intake is equally vital in these cases, as dehydration can exacerbate constipation, creating a cycle of discomfort that is harder to break.

**When to See a Vet**

The decision to seek professional veterinary care hinges on a variety of factors. Chief among them the duration and severity of symptoms. Diarrhea that persists for more than a day, particularly if accompanied by vomiting, lethargy, or a loss of appetite, signals the need for immediate intervention. Constipation, while sometimes resolved with dietary changes, also warrants a vet visit if it persists, to rule out the possibility of obstructions or other underlying conditions that dietary adjustments alone cannot address.

The transition from at-home care to professional intervention should be seamless, with the welfare of the dog as the guiding principle. In these moments, detailed records of the dog's symptoms, dietary history, and any potential incidents that could have precipitated the upset become invaluable, offering the veterinarian a comprehensive view that can aid in diagnosis and treatment.

**Preventive Measures**

Prevention, a cornerstone of managing canine health, plays a critical role in mitigating the risk of future digestive upsets. This proactive approach encompasses a spectrum of strategies, from maintaining a consistent, balanced diet to ensuring regular exercises, which aids in digestive motility and overall gut health.

Mindful monitoring of a dog's environment to prevent dietary indiscretion—securing trash cans, keeping toxic foods out of reach, and supervising outdoor activities—can significantly reduce the incidence of digestive issues. Regular deworming and vaccinations, according to a schedule recommended by a veterinarian, protect against parasites and infections that can disrupt gastrointestinal health.

Incorporating probiotics into the diet, either through specially formulated foods or supplements, can also support a healthy gut microbiome, enhancing digestive function and bolstering the immune system against pathogens that might otherwise lead to upsets.

This layered strategy, embracing both immediate interventions and long-term preventive care, underscores the multifaceted approach required to navigate the complexities of canine digestive health. It's a testament to the understanding that the well-being of our dogs is not solely dependent on how we react to issues as they arise but on how effectively we can prevent them, ensuring a life of comfort, health, and joy for our beloved companions.

## 7.5 TRANSITIONING SENIOR DOGS TO A HOMEMADE DIET

Navigating the nuanced dietary shift to homemade meals for senior dogs requires an understanding that extends beyond simple food preparation. At this stage in their lives, the metabolic intricacies of aging canines demand a diet that not only satisfies their taste buds but also caters to their evolving health needs. The shift towards a homemade diet, rich in nutrients and tailored to individual health profiles, promises a revitalization of both body and spirit, offering our aging companions meals that nourish in every sense.

The dietary needs of senior dogs diverge significantly from those of their younger counterparts, with considerations for caloric intake, nutrient absorption, and digestive efficiency taking precedence. Reduced metabolism and energy levels in older dogs necessitate a careful calibration of calories to prevent unwanted weight gain, a condition that could exacerbate existing health issues such as arthritis or heart disease. Likewise, the prevalence of chronic conditions, including renal insufficiency or liver disease, requires diets formulated to mitigate these concerns, often focusing on reduced protein levels or specific nutrient profiles designed to support organ function.

Transitioning to a homemade diet for senior dogs, therefore, begins with a gentle, thoughtful approach, acknowledging the potential for digestive sensitivities and the importance of maintaining a consistent nutrient intake. The introduction of new meals is gradual, allowing the digestive system to adjust without stress. Initial offerings might blend small portions of homemade food with their usual fare, slowly increasing the homemade portion as tolerance is observed. This method minimizes the risk of gastrointestinal upset, ensuring the transition supports health without causing distress.

The collaboration with a veterinarian throughout this process is indispensable. Their expertise offers insights into the unique health challenges faced by aging canines, guiding the formulation of a diet that addresses these concerns while promoting overall well-being. This partnership ensures that the homemade diet not only meets the general nutritional requirements but also aligns with any medical protocols, integrating seamlessly with treatments for chronic conditions. Regular check-ups and discussions about the dog's response to the new diet facilitate a dynamic approach to meal planning, one that evolves in concert with the dog's changing health landscape.

The commitment to transitioning senior dogs to a homemade diet, infused with patience and underscored by vigilance, reflects a deep-seated respect for their life stage and an acknowledgment of the profound bond shared between pet and owner. It's a testament to the belief that every meal should contribute to a life marked not just by years, but by quality and contentment, ensuring our companions thrive in their golden years.

## 7.6 BALANCING HOMEMADE MEALS WITH OCCASIONAL COMMERCIAL FOODS

Balancing homemade meals with commercial dog foods blends well with nutritional care. This balance, valued for combining ease with nutritional reliability, calls for careful planning to make sure dogs get the full advantages of both diets without losing out on essential nutrients. It's not just about alternating between two types of food but it's about establishing a consistent dietary plan that promotes the well-being and joy of our dogs.

The seamless weaving together of homemade and commercial diets often finds its motivation in the practicalities of modern life, whether due to the demands of travel or the constraints of time, the inclusion of commercial foods can offer a pragmatic solution without veering from the path of nutritional integrity. The key lies in selecting commercial foods that mirrors the quality and composition of their homemade counterparts, ensuring a consistency that the canine digestive system can navigate with ease. In practical terms, this might translate to choosing commercial foods that are free from artificial additives and rich in whole, identifiable ingredients, a reflection of the wholesome meals prepared at home.

Ensuring that the combined diet meets every nutritional requirement of our canine companions extends beyond a mere tally of ingredients. It involves a deep understanding of their unique dietary needs, influenced by factors such as age, activity level, and health status. This comprehensive view allows for the identification of potential gaps in nutrition that might emerge from the combination of homemade and commercial foods. For instance, if a commercial diet forms the baseline, homemade additions might focus on enhancing omega-3 fatty acid intake, using ingredients like flaxseed or salmon, which might be underrepresented in the commercial formula. Conversely, if homemade meals provide the core nutrition, commercial foods can serve as a convenient source of essential vitamins and minerals, ensuring a well-rounded diet.

Selecting high-quality commercial dog foods requires a discerning eye and each choice is governed by rigorous quality criteria. This careful choice goes beyond merely reviewing the list of ingredients to include a thorough assessment of the brand's production methods, the origin of its ingredients and its dedication to nutritional value. Companies that emphasize openness, providing clear explanations of their recipes and ingredient sources, are often the most reliable. This selection process ensures that the commercial food aspects of the diet positively impact your dog's health, offering a convenient yet nutritious complement to the homemade meals you prepare.

Transitioning between homemade and commercial diets, whether due to travel or other life exigencies, demands a strategic approach to avoid digestive disturbances. A gradual introduction, where new foods are slowly integrated over several days, allows the dog's digestive system to adjust without distress. This method not only minimizes the risk of gastrointestinal upset but also provides an opportunity to observe the dog's acceptance and reaction to the new diet. It's a process that underscores the importance of patience and observation, where the dog's well-being serves as the guiding principle in navigating dietary changes.

This chapter seamlessly integrates into the overarching narrative of our guide, highlighting the importance of adaptability, discernment, and thoughtful care in the dietary management and transition strategies for our dogs. These core principles emphasize our dedication to nurturing our dogs' health and happiness through chosen meals. It reflects the deep connection we have with our pets, fueled by our commitment to their well-being. Moving forward, let's apply what we've learned with deliberate care and affection, always bearing in mind the significant role our dietary choices play in enhancing the lives of our beloved dogs.

# CHAPTER 8
# BUILDING A CIRCLE OF
# SUPPORT AND KNOWLEDGE

In the journey of dog ownership, unique experiences weave together, creating a supportive community where stories of friendship, obstacles, and achievements are shared. Embarking on the choice to feed our dogs homemade meals ties us closer, fostering a sense of unity and mutual understanding. This rewarding journey is also filled with challenges that often require the comfort found in togetherness and the insights gained from collective knowledge. It's within this network of fellow dog owners and the advice from experienced professionals that we find guidance, confidently tackling the complexities of homemade canine nutrition together.

## 8.1 FORMING A SUPPORT NETWORK WITH FELLOW DOG OWNERS

### Finding Local and Online Groups

In the same way, a lone wolf finds strength in the pack, and dog owners thrive in the company of others who share their commitment to canine well-being. This search for like-minded individuals leads to local dog parks, where conversations spark over shared interests, or to online forums, where advice and experiences are exchanged across the digital ether. Websites such as Meetup provide a platform for organizing local dog owner groups, offering an array of events from nutrition workshops to group walks, fostering not only companionship among dogs but also a sense of community among owners. Social media platforms and their groups dedicated to pet care, serve as another fertile ground for connection, allowing for the exchange of recipes, tips, and success stories that inspire and guide.

### Benefits of Community

Within this network, the collective wisdom of experienced and novice dog owners alike becomes an invaluable resource. Here, advice on tackling dietary allergies, recommendations for supplementing homemade meals, or strategies for transitioning dogs to new diets circulate with the generosity characteristic of those who have navigated similar paths. This exchange transcends mere information sharing, weaving a safety net that catches us in moments of doubt or difficulty, reminding us that we are not alone in our endeavors.

## Organizing Meet-Ups

The tangible connection fostered through face-to-face interaction enriches this shared journey, transforming abstract exchanges into meaningful relationships. Organizing local meet-ups, perhaps at a dog-friendly café or a community center, offers an arena for live demonstrations on meal preparation, tastings for our canine companions, and discussions on the latest in canine nutrition research. These gatherings, marked by the laughter of owners and the wagging of tails, become milestones that punctuate our calendar, anticipated events that offer both learning and leisure.

## Sharing Success Stories

Amidst this exchange of knowledge and experience, success stories emerge as beacons, illuminating the path for those who follow. An interactive blog or newsletter, contributed to by members of the dog owner community serves as a repository for these tales. Each story, whether it chronicles a dog's recovery from health issues through diet change or celebrates the small victories of a picky eater accepting homemade meals, carries a message of hope and affirmation. These narratives, rich with detail and emotion, not only educate but empower, offering tangible proof of the difference we can make in our dogs' lives.

## Visual Element: Community Recipe Exchange Board

## Community Recipe Exchange Board

Picture a digital bulletin board, a collage of homemade dog food recipes, each accompanied by photos, ingredient lists, and preparation instructions. This interactive platform invites members to submit their dog's favorite recipes, share feedback on trials of others' submissions, and suggest modifications for health conditions or dietary preferences. Such a tool not only enriches the community's culinary repertoire but fosters a spirit of collaboration and creativity, encouraging owners to experiment with new ingredients and techniques, secure in the support and shared knowledge of their peers.

In this collective endeavor, the journey of providing our dogs with nutritious, homemade meals becomes a shared narrative, enriched with the contributions and companionship of fellow dog owners. Our individual efforts, magnified by the strength of community, weave a story of love, dedication, and transformation, a testament to the bonds that unite us in the pursuit of our dogs' health and happiness.

## 8.2 STAYING INFORMED: CONTINUED LEARNING ABOUT CANINE NUTRITION

In the ever-evolving landscape of canine nutrition, the pursuit of knowledge unfolds as a relentless quest, marked not by the attainment of absolute truths but by the continuous accumulation of insights, discoveries, and understandings. This dynamic field, where the boundaries of science and wellness intersect, invites a vigilant eye and an eager mind, for the welfare of our beloved companions hinges upon our capacity to adapt, learn, and apply the burgeoning wealth of information that shapes this discipline.

### Following Canine Nutrition Research

Navigating the maze of canine nutrition research demands a keen sense of curiosity coupled with a discerning approach to the evaluation of new studies, findings, and hypotheses. With every paper published or study released, the foundation of our understanding shifts, subtly or significantly, guiding our decisions and strategies in feeding our dogs. Academic journals, reputable institutions, and conferences dedicated to veterinary science become invaluable resources, offering a window into the cutting-edge of nutritional science. These sources, rich with the potential to alter our perceptions and practices, require a diligent review, where the methodology, sample size, and potential biases are weighed with meticulous care. It is within this careful scrutiny that the veracity of research finds its measure, and its applicability to our dogs' diets is thoughtfully considered.

## Recommended Reading

The compilation of a reading list, curated with precision and care, serves as a beacon for those navigating the vast seas of canine nutrition information. Books penned by experts in veterinary nutrition, articles sourced from esteemed veterinary journals, and guidelines offered by professional associations stand as pillars upon which a robust understanding of dog health and nutrition can be built. Websites endorsed by veterinary professionals offer a stream of accessible yet scientifically grounded content, bridging the gap between academic research and practical application. This list, everexpanding and evolving, becomes a personal library of knowledge, a tool for empowerment in the quest to provide our dogs with the best possible care.

## Attending Seminars and Webinars

The digital age brings with it learning opportunities that transcend geographical boundaries, offering seminars and webinars that connect enthusiasts, professionals, and experts in a virtual symposium of shared knowledge. These events, ranging from introductory courses on canine nutrition to in-depth discussions on specific health conditions, cater to a spectrum of interests and expertise levels. Participation in these educational gatherings not only expands one's knowledge base but also fosters a sense of connection with the broader community of dog nutrition advocates. Each session, whether it delves into the nuances of dietary fats or explores the latest trends in food formulation, contributes to a layered understanding of canine health, equipping attendees with the insights necessary to make informed decisions for their pets.

**Critical Evaluation of Sources**

In an era where information is as abundant as it is varied, the ability to critically assess the reliability and credibility of sources becomes paramount. This skill, honed through practice and guided by a set of criteria, enables the discernment of valuable information from that which is misleading or erroneous. Considerations such as the author's credentials, the publication's reputation, and the presence of citations and references serve as indicators of credibility, filtering the wheat from the chaff in the vast fields of content. Moreover, the examination of opposing viewpoints and the scrutiny of evidence supporting claims illuminate the complexities of canine nutrition, encouraging a balanced and well-informed perspective. Through this rigorous evaluation, the integrity of the information that informs our choices is safeguarded, ensuring that our actions are grounded in knowledge rather than conjecture.

In this pursuit of knowledge, where the only constant is change, our commitment to staying informed becomes a testament to our dedication to the health and happiness of our canine companions. It is a pursuit not of finality but of progression, a continuous journey marked by the acquisition of knowledge, the refinement of beliefs, and the unwavering dedication to the well-being of those who depend on us. The landscape of canine nutrition, rich with complexity and nuance, offers not just challenges but opportunities for growth, learning, and connection. Through this endeavor, we not only enhance the lives of our dogs but enrich our own, bound by the shared goal of nurturing a life of vitality and joy for our beloved pets.

## 8.3 ENGAGING WITH EXPERTS: WHEN TO SEEK PROFESSIONAL ADVICE

In the complex world of dog nutrition, filled with many variables and uncertainties, the expertise of veterinary nutritionists stands out as essential guidance. These experts, armed with extensive knowledge and training, offer deep insights that surpass what most dog owners may know, providing custom advice for the unique dietary needs of each dog. Therefore, consulting with a veterinary nutritionist is not merely an option but a crucial step for anyone committed to enhancing their dog's health with homemade meals.

Collaborating with nutritional experts is like customizing a perfect outfit for your dog, where every detail is tailored to fit. The goal is to create a nutrition plan that matches your dog's specific needs as closely as a custom-fit suit, considering their age, health, breed, and level of activity. The advantages of such tailored advice are extensive, providing not only reassurance but also a detailed guide to achieving nutritional balance and enhancing health. This personalized plan lays the groundwork for your dog's daily meals and nutritional supplements, ensuring each meal is a step towards better health.

Preparation, as in many endeavors, is key to maximizing the benefits of consultations with veterinary nutritionists. Crafting a list of questions before meetings transforms these sessions from general discussions into focused explorations of the dog's nutritional landscape. Inquiries might range from the specifics of dietary adjustments needed to manage certain health conditions to the integration of supplements, or the evaluation of ingredient quality and sources. This premeditated approach ensures that no stone is left unturned, and the advice received is as comprehensive and actionable as possible.

The assembly of a healthcare team for one's dog mirrors the gathering of a council, where each member contributes their expertise towards the common goal of the canine's health. This team might include not only a veterinary nutritionist but also a primary care veterinarian, a holistic veterinary practitioner, and specialists for any health conditions the dog may have. Each professional brings a unique perspective, enriching the collective approach to the dog's care. Regular communication and collaboration among this team ensure that dietary plans remain aligned with the dog's health protocols and that any adjustments are made with a holistic view of the dog's well-being in mind.

This collaborative, informed approach to managing and enhancing a dog's diet through homemade meals underscores a commitment to not just the physical health of the canine companion but also to a deeper understanding of the role nutrition plays in their life. It is an acknowledgment that the path to optimal well-being is a shared one, navigated through the combined efforts of dedicated owners and skilled professionals.

## 8.4 DOCUMENTING YOUR DOG'S DIET AND HEALTH PROGRESS

### Keeping a Food Diary

Keeping a detailed food diary for our dogs is more than a routine task—it's a vital tool that guides us in making informed dietary choices and tracks the impact of diet on their health over time. By consistently recording what our dogs eat, along with portion sizes, reactions, and any noticeable changes in health or behavior, we create a comprehensive resource. This diary, filled out with care each day, evolves into much more than just a collection of notes. It becomes a dynamic record that illuminates the connection between diet and overall well-being, offering valuable insights into the optimal way to nourish our canine friends.

The importance of maintaining a food diary lies in a simple fact: our memories aren't always reliable. Details of everyday feeding can easily merge together, becoming vague and indistinct over time. In contrast, a food diary brings clarity and precision to our dogs' diets. It meticulously records every ingredient, helping to pinpoint those that benefit our pets and those that don't. This diary becomes essential for identifying dietary sensitivities, monitoring nutritional intake, and fine-tuning meal portions. Ultimately, it helps us craft the perfect diet plan for our cherished dogs, based on accurate, detailed information gathered over time.

## Sharing with Healthcare Professionals

Having the food diary, conversations with veterinarians and nutritionists become significantly more detailed, shifting towards custom-tailored care. This detailed record enables a deeper, more meaningful dialogue, offering a clear chronology of dietary shifts and their impacts on health. With the expertise of these professionals, the diary evolves into a crucial diagnostic instrument, with each entry contributing to a fuller picture of your dog's nutritional health.

For the veterinary nutritionist, the food diary acts as a foundational tool. It allows for the creation of a customized diet plan, meticulously informed by the dog's recorded dietary history. Through discussions informed by the diary's contents, dietary adjustments are made with unmatched accuracy, each change a deliberate move toward peak health. In this context, the food diary serves as a crucial link, turning anecdotal evidence into concrete data, leading to informed, effective dietary decisions.

## Celebrating Milestones

The food diary stands as a record of milestones, each achievement in health and well-being a cause for celebration beyond its utility as a tool for dietary management and communication. These moments, captured in the diary's entries, serve as markers of progress, reminders of the journey traveled from uncertainty to assurance. They are the first successful introduction of a novel protein after months of allergic reactions, the visible improvement in vitality following a dietary adjustment, or the day-to-day joys of a dog fully engaged with their meals.

These milestones, chronicled with care, offer not just a record of progress but a source of motivation, a tangible reminder of the impact of our efforts. They underscore the value of the food diary not just as a logistical tool but as an emotional ledger, capturing the highs and lows of the journey towards optimal canine health.

In this practice of meticulous documentation, the food diary transcends its initial function, becoming a cornerstone of canine care. It reflects a commitment to understanding and optimizing the role of diet in our dogs' lives, an affirmation of the belief that the best care is informed, intentional, and individualized. Through this lens, the diary is not just a collection of entries but a manifestation of love, a testament to the lengths we will go to ensure the health and happiness of our canine companions.

## 8.5 ADVOCATING FOR WHOLE FOODS: EDUCATING OTHERS ON HOMEMADE DOG FOOD BENEFITS

Moving towards a whole-food diet highlights our growing understanding of how crucial nutrition is for our dogs' health and longevity in the canine care. This change, though increasingly popular among dog owners, faces resistance due to long-standing myths and misconceptions about homemade dog food. Advocating for this dietary choice goes beyond simple preference, becoming a mission to educate and convince others of the benefits of whole foods, using solid evidence, personal stories, and educational efforts.

The advocacy is rooted in highlighting the numerous advantages that whole foods provide to our dogs. Central to this is the focus on minimally processed ingredients which ensure that our pets get their nutrients in the most natural and readily absorbable forms. This diet supports optimal digestion, crucial for health as the gastrointestinal system plays a key role in absorbing nutrients and supporting immune health. Additionally, the abundance of antioxidants in fresh fruits and vegetables acts as a natural shield against oxidative stress, thereby lowering the risk of chronic illnesses and bolstering cellular health. The diverse range of ingredients in a whole foods diet also guarantees a well-rounded nutrient intake, preventing the nutritional gaps that can occur with more uniform diets.

Addressing the prevailing misconceptions about homemade dog food necessitates a careful deconstruction of the myths that cloud public perception. Foremost among these is the belief that homemade diets inherently lack nutritional completeness. This argument, though rooted in concern for canine well-being, dismisses the capacity of well-researched, carefully crafted whole-food diets to meet and often exceed the nutritional benchmarks set by commercial foods. Another common misconception posits that preparing homemade dog food is excessively time-consuming and financially burdensome. Countering this narrative involves not only highlighting the efficiency of batch cooking and the cost-effectiveness of purchasing ingredients in bulk but also emphasizing the long-term health benefits that can lead to reduced veterinary costs.

The dissemination of educational resources plays a crucial role in shifting the tide of opinion towards a more favorable view of homemade dog food. Crafting leaflets that distill the science behind canine nutrition into accessible language, conducting workshops that demonstrate the simplicity and joy of preparing whole food meals, or producing videos that showcase the vibrancy and health of dogs thriving on these diets are all strategies that serve to demystify and promote this dietary approach. These materials, shared through social media, community bulletin boards, or veterinary offices, become conduits of knowledge, sparking curiosity and encouraging informed dialogue among dog owners.

The most potent form of advocacy resides in the living examples provided by our dogs themselves. The transformation in health and vitality that accompanies a shift to a whole-food diet often speaks louder than any pamphlet or workshop. A coat that gleams with health, eyes that sparkle with energy, and a vitality that radiates from within serve as compelling endorsements of the diet's efficacy. These visible changes, coupled with stories of improved health outcomes, reduced allergies, and enhanced quality of life, offer tangible proof of the benefits that whole foods can provide. Sharing these success stories, whether through personal conversations, social media posts, or participation in community events, not only validates the choice of a whole-food diet but also inspires others to consider this path for their own canine companions.

In this endeavor of advocacy, the goal is not merely to persuade but to enlighten, offering dog owners the knowledge and confidence to explore whole-food diets as a viable and beneficial option for their pets. It is an invitation to join a movement that seeks not just to feed but to nourish, ensuring that our dogs live not only longer lives but also ones filled with health, joy, and vitality.

## 8.6 EXPLORING ADVANCED CANINE NUTRITION COURSES AND RESOURCES

Delving into structured learning environments focused on canine nutrition can greatly enhance one's grasp and implementation of diet principles specifically designed for our dogs. This quest for deeper knowledge is more than just academic—it's a commitment to the health and welfare of our pets, aiming to provide them with diets that not only extend their lives but also ensure they are filled with vitality and well-being.

## Sources for Finding Advanced Courses

The quest for advanced courses in canine nutrition unveils a plethora of options, from academic institutions offering specialized programs to online platforms hosting a range of courses designed for varied levels of expertise. Esteemed universities have begun to recognize the growing interest in pet health, subsequently developing curricula that address both foundational and advanced aspects of canine nutrition. These courses, often taught by leading researchers and practitioners in the field, combine rigorous scientific study with practical dietary management strategies. Additionally, professional organizations dedicated to veterinary nutrition frequently host workshops and seminars, providing opportunities for immersive learning experiences. Digital platforms such as Coursera and Udemy also serve as gateways to courses curated by experts, offering the flexibility of self-paced study alongside the depth of specialized knowledge.

## Certification Programs

Certification programs in canine nutrition present an opportunity to achieve professional recognition for those inclined towards a more formalized path of education,. These programs, structured to impart a comprehensive understanding of canine dietary needs, metabolic disorders, and the impact of nutrition on behavior and longevity, culminate in certification that attests to the holder's expertise. Institutions offering these certifications maintain rigorous standards, ensuring that graduates are well-equipped to advise on canine nutrition, whether in a professional capacity or as informed guardians of their pets. Completing a certification program not only enhances personal knowledge but also establishes credibility, facilitating a role as a trusted advisor within the dog owner community.

**Online Resources and Communities**

The digital age has ushered in an era where information and community support are but a click away. Websites dedicated to canine health, forums populated by dog nutrition enthusiasts, and social media groups offer a wealth of resources for ongoing learning. These platforms encourage the exchange of the latest research findings, discussions on emerging trends in dog diets, and the sharing of personal experiences with various nutritional approaches. The interactive nature of these communities fosters a dynamic learning environment, where questions are posed, debates are had, and insights are gained in real time. Engaging with these online resources and communities not only broadens one's understanding of canine nutrition but also embeds individuals within a network of support, where collective wisdom bolsters personal knowledge.

# PLEASE HELP ANOTHER DOG LOVER!

**Please help another dog lover by giving this book a little bark of your own.**

**Just scan the QR Code to share your thoughts:**

Please submit a photo of your dog wearing a bandana around their neck with your Amazon Review of my cookbook. I would love to see all of your beautiful dogs ready to eat some 'Healthy Homemade Dog Food'. I'm sure the rest of the world would love to see them also😊

# CONCLUSION

As we come to the close of this journey together, I'm reminded of the profound transformation that awaits you and your beloved canine companion. From the first page to the last, we've ventured through the vast landscape of homemade dog nutrition, navigating the nuances of what it truly means to nourish our dogs from the bowl up. It's been a pathway to empowerment, a means to forge an even deeper bond with our four-legged family members through the very act of care in their meals.

Reflecting on the importance of fresh, whole foods for our dogs, it's clear the impact that such a diet can have on their well-being. The gleam in their coat, the vigor in their step, and the brightness in their eyes are testaments to the vitality that whole foods can bring. Oral hygiene, healthier skin, a shiny coat, and an overall boost in longevity aren't just hopes; they're tangible outcomes of the recipes and methods we've shared.

I hope I've managed to demystify the process, showing you that creating wholesome, homemade meals for your dog doesn't require a chef's expertise or a bottomless wallet. With a bit of planning, some savvy shopping, and a sprinkle of creativity, you can provide your dog with meals that are not only nutritious but also cost-effective and simple to prepare.

This book, with its detailed nutrient and calorie charts, the 4-week transition guide, and suggestions for addressing specific health concerns through diet, was crafted to be your compass in the kitchen. It's a tool, yes, but also a companion on this journey towards a healthier, happier life for your dog.

I encourage you to take that first step, to experiment with the recipes and harness the strategies we've discussed. Remember, even small shifts in your dog's diet can make a world of difference in their health and happiness. You don't have to be perfect; you just have to start.

Let's not forget, that at the heart of this book is a shared love for our dogs, a love that was embodied by my faithful friend, Sundance. It's this love that motivates us to seek out the best care for them, to ensure they live not just long lives but lives filled with joy and good health.

I invite you to join the vibrant community of dog owners who have embarked on this homemade meal journey. Share your stories, your successes, and even your flops. There's a wealth of support and friendship waiting in online forums and local groups, where our collective wisdom can grow and flourish.

And as you continue on this path, keep the spirit of learning alive. Canine nutrition is an ever-evolving field, and there's always more to discover. Don't hesitate to consult with veterinarians or canine nutritionists, to tailor your dog's diet to their unique needs. It's a step that Sundance taught me is invaluable.

In closing, I hope Sundance's legacy and the pages of this book inspire you as much as he inspired me. If we've managed to guide you even a step further in the journey of providing better nutrition for your dog, then we've succeeded in our mission. Here's to the many meals and memories you'll create with your dog, each one a step towards a healthier, happier life together. Cheers to you and your furry companion, on this journey of love, care, and nourishment.

# REFERENCES

- *Nutritional Needs for Different Dog Ages* https://www.hillspet.com/dog-care/routine-care/needs-of-adult-dogs
- *How to Read a Dog Food Label - WebMD* https://www.webmd.com/pets/dogs/features/how-to-read-a-dog-food-label
- *Homemade Dog Food Recipes: Choosing Balanced Ingredients* https://www.akc.org/expert-advice/nutrition/choosing-ingredients-homemade-dog-food/
- *Food Allergies in Dogs - VCA Animal Hospitals* https://vcahospitals.com/know-your-pet/food-allergies-in-dogs
- *20 Essential Tools and Equipment - Daily Dog Food Recipes* https://dailydogfoodrecipes.com/tools-and-equipment/
- *A Beginner's Guide to Home Cooking for Dogs* https://unionlakeveterinaryhospital.com/blog/a-beginners-guide-to-home-cooking-for-dogs
- *undefined* undefined
- *Homemade Dog Food: Vet-Approved Recipes For Dogs* https://www.thewildest.com/dog-nutrition/vet-approved-homemade-dog-food
- *Homemade Dog Food Recipes: Choosing Balanced ...* https://www.akc.org/expert-advice/nutrition/choosing-ingredients-homemade-dog-food/
- *Buying Dog Food In Bulk: Benefits & Risks* https://www.dogster.com/dog-nutrition/buying-dog-food-in-bulk
- *Keep Food Safe! Food Safety Basics* http://www.fsis.usda.gov/food-safety/safe-food-handling-and-preparation/food-safety-basics/steps-keep-food-safe
- *DIY Dog Meal Prep Tips* https://www.justfoodfordogs.com/blog/diy-dog-meal-prep-hacks.html
- *Should You Make Homemade Dog Food?* https://www.webmd.com/pets/dogs/features/homemade-dog-food
- *How To Choose The Best Protein For Your Dogs* https://www.wellnesspetfood.com/blog/how-to-choose-the-best-protein-for-your-dogs/
- *Role of Dietary Fatty Acids in Dogs & Cats* https://todaysveterinarypractice.com/nutrition/role-of-dietary-fatty-acids-in-dogs-cats/
- *Fruits and Vegetables Dogs Can or Can't Eat* https://www.akc.org/expert-advice/nutrition/fruits-vegetables-dogs-can-and-cant-eat/
- *9 Best Anti-Inflammatory Foods for Dogs to Boost Their Health* https://www.justfoodfordogs.com/blog/anti-inflammatory-foods-for-dogs.html

- *Your Guide to Prebiotics & Probiotics for Dogs - Bold by Nature* https://boldbynature.com/blog/your-guide-to-prebiotics-probiotics-for-dogs/
- *Importance of Antioxidants for Dogs | Vetericyn* https://vetericyn.com/blog/importance-of-antioxidants-for-dogs/
- *Should You Naturally Detox Your Pet? Benefits and Risks ...* https://raisingyourpetsnaturally.com/pet-detox/
- *Superfoods For Dogs — Elite Veterinary Care* https://www.eliteveterinarycare.com/blog/superfoods-for-dogs-12-healthful-snacks-you-can-share-with-your-pup
- *The Pros and Cons of Fermented Foods For Dogs* https://www.dogsnaturallymagazine.com/fermented-veggies-why-dead-is-best/
- *14 Best Herbs for Dogs - Guide to Health Benefits* https://www.bonza.dog/2023/07/best-herbs-for-dogs-health/
- *Prebiotics and Probiotics for Dogs and Cats* https://todaysveterinarynurse.com/nutrition/prebiotics-and-probiotics-for-dogs-and-cats/
- *Vet-Approved Homemade Dog Food Recipes* https://www.thesprucepets.com/homemade-dog-food-recipes-5200240
- *undefined* undefined
- *Homemade Dog Food Recipe for Skin Allergies (Vet ...* https://holisticvetblend.com/blogs/news/homemade-dog-food-recipe-for-skin-allergies-vet-approved
- *Our Favorite Homemade Dog Food Recipes for Senior Dogs* https://dogquality.com/blogs/senior-dog-blog/our-favorite-homemade-dog-food-recipes-for-senior-dogs
- *Homemade Dog Food Forum* https://www.dogfoodadvisor.com/forums/forum/homemade-dog-food/
- *Emerging topics in nutrition: See latest research in JAVMA* https://www.avma.org/blog/emerging-topics-nutrition-see-latest-research-javma
- *What Is a Veterinary Nutritionist, and Does My Dog Need to ...* https://www.dailypaws.com/dogs-puppies/dog-nutrition/what-is-a-veterinary-nutritionist
- *Effects of a whole food diet on immune function and ...* https://www.frontiersin.org/articles/10.3389/fvets.2022.898056

Made in United States
Orlando, FL
16 November 2024

53988834R00093